WILD RIDE

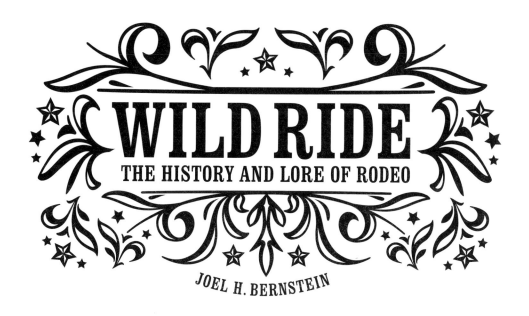

WILD RIDE

THE HISTORY AND LORE OF RODEO

JOEL H. BERNSTEIN

Gibbs Smith, Publisher

TO ENRICH AND INSPIRE HUMANKIND

Salt Lake City | Charleston | Santa Fe | Santa Barbara

**To my parents, Adeline and Leonard "Sonny" Bernstein,
to my wife, Gail, and to all the cowboys and cowgirls who
have helped to preserve so much of our heritage**

First Edition
11 10 09 08 07   5 4 3 2 1

Text © 2007 Joel H. Bernstein
Photographs courtesy of the Dickinson Research Center at the National Cowboy &
Western Heritage Museum, Oklahoma, OK, on pages 12–13, 17, 24, 27, 32, 37, 58, 61, 63,
65, 67, 71, 72, 79, 97, 98, 104, 107, 128, 135, 160, 162, 164, and 165

Published by
Gibbs Smith, Publisher
P.O. Box 667
Layton, Utah 84041

Orders: 1.800.835.4993
www.gibbs-smith.com

Designed by Blackeye Design
Printed and bound in China
Library of Congress Cataloging-in-Publication Data

Bernstein, Joel H.
  Wild ride : the history and lore of rodeo / Joel Bernstein. — 1st ed.
    p. cm.
  ISBN-13: 978-1-58685-745-5
  ISBN-10: 1-58685-745-2
  1. Rodeos—History. 2. Rodeos—Folklore. I. Title.

GV1834.5.B46 2007
791.8'409—dc22

2006030678

⋖ Table of Contents ⋗

❖ Acknowledgments ❖

First and foremost, I owe the completion of this book to my wife, Gail. Using my computer really does pose a problem for me, and without Gail and her unlimited patience, I'd still be cursing at a machine.

The Professional Rodeo Cowboys Association could not have been more helpful. Without the support and guidance of Sherry Compton in Media Relations and Ludell Walter, at the ProRodeo Hall of Fame, this entire project would still be in the planning stages.

To all the other associations, including the Canadian Professional Rodeo Association, National Intercollegiate Rodeo Association, Senior Pro Rodeo, Women's Professional Rodeo Association, National Little Britches Rodeo Association, Professional Bull Riders, the All Indian Rodeo Association, American Junior Rodeo Association, National High School Rodeo Association, Miss Rodeo America, and the *ProRodeo Sports News*, thanks for your help and quick responses to my questions and requests for photos and information.

To all the cowboys and cowgirls who so generously sent me photos and had good conversations with me on the phone, I hope this book conveys all the history and traditions that you so clearly represent to me.

To Louise Serpa of Tucson, one of the great rodeo-arena photographers, thanks for inviting me to your home and sharing wonderful stories and some of the best rodeo photographs I have ever seen.

Thanks to my good friends Paul Zarzyski and Ian Tyson, whose words and music keep alive a tradition and way of life that we all cherish and fortunately have been part of.

To Lewis Bowman, who was there when the Turtles were founded, thanks for supplying me with stories and character studies that would be hard to find anywhere else.

Thanks to George Myren, my friend in Edmonton, Alberta, who helped me with insights into the Canadian circuit and some good photographs. He is in the Canadian Hall of Fame.

A big thanks to someone I've never met, Kendra Santos, whose work as an editor of the *ProRodeo Sports News* and columns for *America Cowboy Magazine* have always been insightful and entertaining.

And finally, I'd like to share my admiration and respect for all the competitors out there, past and present, amateur and pro, who keep rodeo alive and share their way of life with a worldwide audience. It has been an honor and a pleasure to write about you.

☆ Ride 'em

Since the competition was held early in the morning before the main show, ropers wait their turn during slack. There is usually slack when too many contestants are in a particular event. Photo courtesy of Louise L. Serpa, Tucson, Arizona.

Cowboy ★

The word *rodeo* (not *ro-DAY-o*) comes from the Spanish and translates into either "roundup" or "gather together." It's a word that identifies a truly American sport. But the word *rodeo* wasn't even used for cowboy contests until 1916. It wasn't, for example, used at the Prescott Frontier Days until 1924, although the rodeo itself dates back to 1888. For more than a hundred years, cowboys and cowgirls have been riding, roping, and romantically reliving life the way many of them imagined it was in the post–Civil War period in the American West. This was the same period that saw the designated *cowboy* become part of the popular vernacular used for anyone in the West who worked with cattle from the back of a horse. Up until that time, drovers walked behind the cattle and poked them with sticks—thus the origins of the term *cowpoke*.

Rodeo, as it developed into a legitimate competition—a real sport—eventually caught on and in a big way. Today more than twenty-four million people go to Professional Rodeo Cowboys Association (PRCA) rodeos in the United States and Canada, and to the surprise of many sports fans, that puts rodeo attendance ahead of such well-known professional sports as golf and tennis, making it the seventh ranked of all professional sports. And those numbers don't even include the more than sixty million fans who tune in to watch the cowboys and cowgirls—and more recently the bull riders—on television from the comfort of their own homes. Rodeos air on OLN, ESPN, ESPN2, CBS, and NBC.

People, whether they are Americans or not, don't seem to be able to erase the picture of the North American cowboy from their own consciousness. Even today, in this very technological world, one of the most enduring images of America is that of the Western landscape with a cowboy riding hard and true on a wild bucking horse in some of the most rugged and beautiful country the mind can conjure up. The cowboy and the bronc—Wyoming has even chosen to honor that image on its license plates.

Scholars have examined the phenomenon of the cowboy ad nauseam; pop culture gurus have tried to explain it and bring it into today's cultural environment; writers have looked at it from every angle. Even economists are fascinated by the sport that grew out of an industry—the range cattle industry. Rodeo has done as much as any one event or one series of events to influence the American imagination and to reinforce the image of the rugged, range cowboy as part of our contemporary culture. To many of their fans, the rodeo cowboy is about the only real, living cowboy they will ever see.

To this day, the cowboy remains an important image for both marketing and America. As recently as 2006 the staid PBS created a new slogan, "Unleash Your Inner Cowboy," to help promote a television series about the West. The series has programs that range from a show about cattle, to a look at Annie Oakley and Buffalo Bill's Wild West Show, to an eight-hour reenactment of 1867 ranch life called *Texas Ranch House*. There is also an hour about the relationship between John Wayne and the director John Ford, and the classic westerns they made together.

Western clothing never seems to go out of style. Dude ranching continues to flourish and, in fact, to grow, making it possible for people who have never been on a ranch, never been *near* a ranch, or never even lived in ranch country, to at least be a small part of what many consider the most American of American experiences. Dude ranches, or guest ranches as they're now called, frequently advertise themselves as working cattle ranches in an attempt to make the experience even more realistic or maybe just a bit more romantic.

ABOVE: Rodeo, New Mexico, was an important shipping point for numerous livestock operations in the area. They took the name *rodeo*, which is the Spanish word for "roundup" or "enclosure." The town is located in extreme southwestern New Mexico, on the Arizona border. Photo courtesy of the author.

For those of us who don't get enough "cowboy," there is also a cable TV channel called Encore Westerns that broadcasts old and new cowboy movies twenty-four hours a day, 365 days a year—and as they trumpet, they are "All western—all the time. Heroic. Rugged." It's surprising to realize how many cowboy movies have actually been made. In *The Westerns: From Silents to the Seventies*, the authors write: "There will always be an audience for the Western, for the Western represents romantic adventure and idealism, achievement, optimism for the future, justice, idealism, the beauty of the land, and the courage and independence of the individuals who won the land." The cowboys and cowgirls of modern rodeo are representative of some of the same traits, particularly "the courage and independence of the individuals" and today have much of the same appeal. Even in this day and age, the word *independent*, more than any other, describes the rodeo cowboy and the life he lives.

In 2004, there were PRCA rodeos in 41 states and 4 Canadian provinces that accounted for 1,982 performances at 671 individual rodeos. The total purse had swelled to well over 35 million dollars. In addition to the elite professional circuit of the PRCA, there are countless amateur, semipro, high school, college, and even prison

Cowgirl relay races at a Tex Austin Rodeo in Chicago, 1927. This was one of the most exciting and entertaining of the women's events.

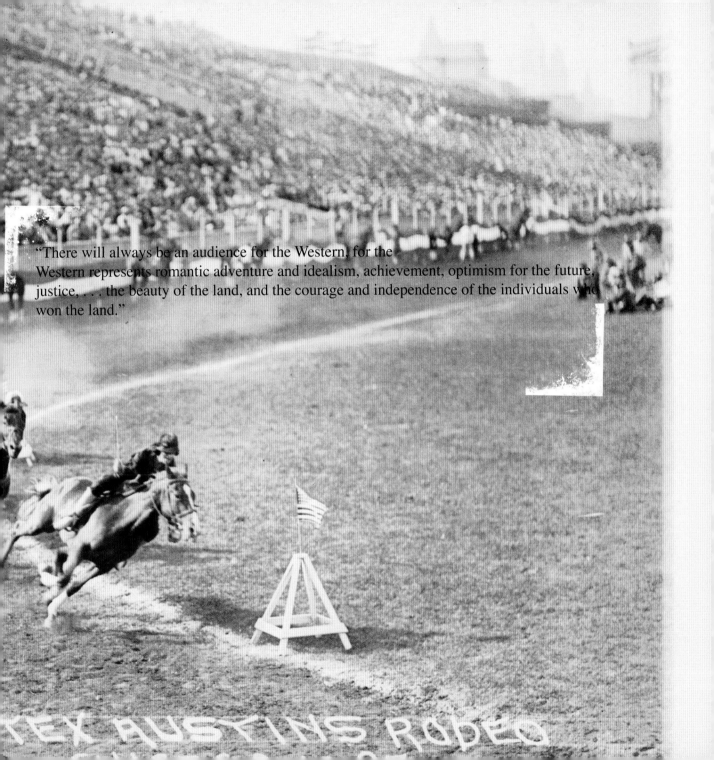

"There will always be an audience for the Western, for the Western represents romantic adventure and idealism, achievement, optimism for the future, justice, . . . the beauty of the land, and the courage and independence of the individuals who won the land."

RIGHT: Four young rodeo contestants spend a little time getting to know one another. They are decked out in chaps and spurs, with gear bags at the ready. This photo is from 1993. Courtesy of Louise L. Serpa, Tucson, Arizona.

BELOW, RIGHT: All Indian National Finals Rodeo, 1976, held in Salt Lake City, Utah. Dan Hall rides the bareback hores "Alley Cat." Photo of James Fain, courtesy of the PRCA.

the richest of all Indian rodeos. More recently, a nationwide Senior Pro Rodeo tour has been created for cowboys and cowgirls over forty years old who compete for prize money that now totals well into the millions. Many of these competitors were professional competitors earlier in their careers.

One of the fastest-growing competitions is the ranch rodeo, for working cowhands, where a group of cowboys and cowgirls represent their particular ranch rather

rodeos. There is even the Professional Armed Forces Rodeo Association composed of cowboys who are now serving in the military. Various state rodeo associations exist, like the New Mexico Rodeo Association and the Montana Rodeo Association. If the Professional Rodeo Cowboys Association is the major leagues, the various state associations are like their AA or AAA farm teams. The money in the state associations can be pretty good, although it varies from state to state, and there are weekly jackpots all over the country. But usually the competitors in these associations compete as an avocation rather than as a full-time profession.

More than one hundred rodeos exist for the youngsters, like the Little Britches events for boys and girls ages eight to eighteen. There is also a full schedule for North American Indians in their own association; this group holds their finals at places like the San Carlo Apache Reservation in southern Arizona and Albuquerque, and they produce the Navajo Nation Fair Rodeo,

1976 ALL INDIAN NATIONAL FINALS RODEO SALT LAKE CITY ©JAMES FAIN PHOTO-LOGAN, UTAH Don Hall "Alley Cat" (Kezby) 5th Go

than themselves. Ranch rodeos are as close as rodeo comes to being a team sport.

Another important group is the Women's Professional Rodeo Association (WPRA) and its affiliate, the All Women's Rodeo, where the gals are trying to reclaim some of the excitement women brought to the rodeo arena in the early part of the twentieth century.

One of the newest and most successful additions to the rodeo world is the Professional Bull Riders (PBR) tour that has captured the imagination and enthusiasm of people all over North America. Participants in the PBR perform before sold-out crowds from the Atlantic to the Pacific.

It's very difficult to get a handle on the untold number of small, local rodeo associations and clubs that meet once a week or once a month for practice or to safely teach youngsters the funda-

mentals of the various competitive events. Sometimes entire towns and villages are involved at the local community arena.

Rodeo has become so universal that it is no longer just a western sport. The Northeast, the South, the Midwestern states—all are fertile grounds for aspiring rodeo cowboys and cowgirls. Even on the pro tours, the contests are held in just about every state in America and the western Canadian provinces. The tours not only bring together cowboys and cowgirls from all over the circuit, but also encourage the locals to enter (and they often do well). In addition to the western states, there are rodeos in states like Alabama, Delaware, Indiana, Virginia, Maryland, Tennessee, and Wisconsin, as well as others that are not generally considered part of the traditional western, cowboy culture. But out in cowboy land, both Wyoming and North Dakota have designated rodeo as their official state sport.

BELOW: The branding event at a ranch rodeo in 1994. Photo courtesy of Louise L. Serpa, Tucson, Arizona.

RIGHT: Ticket for a PRCA rodeo in 2005, held on the Mescalero Apache Indian Reservation. Courtesy of the author.

Inn of the Mountain Gods
PRO RODEO
Mescalero, NM
Sunday Sept. 4th, 2005 @3:30pm
Adult $10
PRCA Sanctioned event
General Gate Admission • Open Seating
0930

Stay at Inn of the Mountain Gods Resort & Casino for two consecutive nights and receive
One Night Free!
Inn of the
MOUNTAIN GODS
RESORT & CASINO
Offer expires November 15, 2005. Free night may be used upon qualification or in prior to expiration date. Blackout dates may apply. Availability must be confirmed at time of reservation. Call 1-800-545-9011 to execute offer.
0930

ABOVE: The 2006 Miss Rodeo America, Colorado cowgirl Tressie Knowlton of Fowler, served the PRCA in a promotional capacity. She traveled over 100,000 miles and appeared at more than 100 rodeos. Tressie grew up on a ranch and trains horses, is proficient at roping and cutting, and helps at the family ranch brandings. She graduated from the University of Colorado with a degree in broadcast journalism. The 2006 pageant was the 51st Miss Rodeo America pageant. Photo courtesy of Miss Rodeo America, Inc., Pueblo, Colorado.

Rodeo isn't a summer sport or a seasonal sport either; it is a year-round competition that culminates in its own national finals in Las Vegas, Nevada, early in December, where the year's champions are crowned in front of sold-out crowds. This is rodeo's World Series. It's the cowboy's Super Bowl. Another aspect of rodeo that is alive and well is the Miss Rodeo America pageant that is held in conjunction with the Wrangler National Finals Rodeo each year. The winner is a spokesperson for rodeo, representing the sport and traveling over 100,000 miles to visit more than 100 rodeos.

None of this came about easily and there were some very hard times, especially in the 1930s, when cowboys actually had to go on strike to make sure that rodeo would endure, continue to grow, and give fair treatment to the cowboys who had committed such a large part of their lives to the sport.

Origins of Rodeo ◆ The historians of rodeo agree that rodeo probably had its origins on July 4, 1869, when several groups of cowboys from nearby ranches got together in Deer Trail, in the northeast part of Colorado, to settle an argument over which cowboys were the best at doing the everyday chores required of ranch hands. This is generally considered the first rodeo, or at least the first recorded one. In the nearly 145 years since Deer Trail, after many trials and tribulations, the sport has grown into what the PRCA calls "the true American sport." It is filled with a colorful history and an equally colorful number of legends that include cowboys, cowgirls, and many of the animals—especially horses and bulls—that they competed with and against. But it wasn't necessarily like that at the outset.

The organizers of the Cheyenne Frontier Days observed that the lifestyle of the cowboys was fading "like the dissolving views of memory." Organizers all over the country tried to bring the lifestyle of the cowboy into the arena. If you've never seen a rodeo you might not fully appreciate that life inside the arena can be just as pun-

The appeal of rodeo, together with its history and romance, pervades just about all levels of American society.

ABOVE: Homer Pettigrew, from Grady, New Mexico, was All-Around Cowboy and six-times steer-wrestling champion. Here he bulldogs at Cheyenne in 1955. Pettigrew was inducted into the ProRodeo Hall of Fame in 1979.

ishing and certainly as dangerous as the cowboy's job is, even today, out on the open range and on the trail.

Competing cowboys and cowgirls have come from all over North America and more recently they have also come in significant numbers from Australia, Mexico, and Brazil. The PBR have even opened offices in Canada, Mexico, Australia, and Brazil to accommodate their own members and growing audience.

The appeal of rodeo, together with its history and romance, pervades just about all levels of American society. The PRCA membership includes about 7,500 cowboys—cowboys who compete in professional rodeo for a living, as well as those who have jobs during the week and compete on the weekends as an avocation. Doctors, lawyers, school teachers, actors, writers, truck drivers, ranchers, TV personalities, and contestants from just about any career you can imagine compete in rodeo events. The women's association has about 2,000 active contestants with just as much diversity, and there are

Hubbell Photo 88

more than 700 members of the PBR, an organization owned and operated by the cowboys themselves.

The PRCA proudly points out that although the cowboys of today are a "bit different" from the cowboys of the past, the "ideals and showmanship of long ago are still valued by today's competitors." The skills needed in the rodeo arena have stayed fairly constant, as has the cowboy code that even today dictates "that a man help his fellow competitors, even though they might be competing for the same paycheck." And that is not just hyperbole—anyone close to rodeo, anyone who has an opportunity to be behind the bucking chutes or watch the ropers as they position their horses in the roping box, will see this part of the rodeo and the cowboy's commitment to the code repeated time and time again. It's just a way of life that they all believe in.

Fierce competitors will regularly be seen helping each other, either lending equipment, horses, or just sharing information about a particular bull, steer, or horse. For example, in July 2005, Ricky Canton of Navasota, Texas, broke the world record for tie-down roping with a run of 6.3 seconds at the Strathmore (Alberta) Stampede. His record-setting run was made on fellow roper Houston Hutto's horse, "Jughead."

Rodeo cowboys keep a "book" on bucking horses and bulls the same way a major league baseball pitcher keeps a "book" on opposing hitters. And they share this information freely. Because so many of the cowboys travel together—they call one another traveling partners—the camaraderie on the circuit, particularly on the pro circuit,

is one of the things that distinguishes rodeo from almost any other professional sport. Traveling partners usually compete in the same events; bareback riders travel together, bull riders travel together, you get the idea. So it's not uncommon for the guy you are traveling with to also be the cowboy who beats you out of a paycheck. The same is true for the barrel racers and the gals in the Women's Professional Rodeo Association (WPRA).

A very positive aspect of this—and a quality very interesting to watch because it seems to be so radically different from other professional sports—is how these same attitudes trickle down to the youngest rodeo contestants, all the way down to the youngsters of the Little Britches rodeos. Cowboys have taken their responsibility as role models very seriously over the years. It is not surprising that today's competitors have so much knowledge about and respect for the past generations of cowboys and cowgirls. Louise Serpa, one of the finest rodeo photographers and the first woman sanctioned by the Rodeo Cowboys Association (RCA) to photograph inside the arena, says in her book *Rodeo* that rodeo has "a kind of sportsmanship found in no other sport." Serpa knows rodeo and the cowboys as well as anyone after spending decades photographing every part of the sport from inside a variety of arenas. In 1999 she was inducted into the National Cowgirl Hall of Fame in Fort Worth, Texas.

OPPOSITE: Cody Lambert of Henrietta, Texas, a good all-around cowboy and a NFR contestant in the bull riding on the Burns Rodeo Company's saddle bronc horse, "Sombrero" in 1988 at Douglas, Wyoming. Photo by Hubbell, courtesy of the Professional Rodeo Cowboys Association.

Post–Civil War ✦ Immediately after the Civil War there were about 500,000 unbranded, wild cattle roaming free on the ranges of Texas that had to be gathered, branded, and shipped. It's been estimated, for example, that the herds on the Texas coastal plains reproduced so fast that every four years the size of the herd doubled. The young men who were able to gather, brand, and ship these herds were all part of the growing cowboy legend. As Walter Prescott Webb explains in *The Great Frontier*, "It was the *method* of handling cattle in this vast pasture that distinguished the ranch cattle business of the Great Plains from the grow- ing of cows around the farmsteads of the eastern part of the United States. The Cattle Kingdom had its birth at the spot where men began to handle cattle on horseback on an open range instead of on foot in small pastures and cow lots." Those young men, a varied mixture of teenagers, black ex-slaves and their descendants, and Mexican vaqueros—the first true western cowboys—have been referred to as "uncommon men," although they were often barely older than boys. Most were just between their late teens and their early twenties and because of the nature of the work (primarily the isolation and the danger) they were usually unmarried. They learned their skills in the early roundups and out on the open range, and most were not a bit hesitant about showing off their skills, particularly when it came to working with cattle or horses.

The West as we have come to know it was brought to the public decades ago by Republic Studios, in the films of directors like John Ford and Sam Peckinpah, and more recently in the films of Clint Eastwood and Kevin Costner. The characters portrayed by classic western stars such as John Wayne, Randolph Scott, Jimmy Stewart, Glenn Ford, Gary Cooper, and Henry Fonda, and the television series as varied as *Rawhide*, *Gunsmoke*, and *The Virginian*, only enhanced the idealistic image of the cowboy. Rodeo was not left out. Hollywood produced some pretty realistic and colorful rodeo movies such as *Junior Bonner*, *The Lusty Men*, and *J. W. Coop*, which premiered in Oklahoma City at the National Finals Rodeo in 1971. These and other rodeo films all added to the image of the professional traveling cowboy. In 1962, TV brought *Stoney Burke* (starring Jack Lord as a saddle bronc rider chasing the world championship) and *The Wide Country* (starring Earl Holliman and Andrew Prine) into America's living rooms. Holliman played Mitch Guthrie, "a world cham-

Professional Bull Riders (PBR) ✦ The PBR is a sort of new cowboy on the block. It was founded in 1992 by twenty successful professional bull riders who took a big risk when they decided to try and make bull riding a "stand-alone" sport. Each of the twenty chipped in $1,000 to get the bull riding organization launched. When the first PBR World Champion, Adriano Moraes of Cachoeira, Brazil, was crowned in 1994, the PBR's main tour consisted of 8 events that offered a total of $250,000 in prize money. They now proclaim themselves as "The Toughest Sport on Dirt," and they promote and sanction over 120 events and draw a live audience of over 1,000,000 in the United States alone. The PBR also has events in Canada, Brazil, and Australia. PBR events on NBC and OLN also reach forty countries around the world and more than 320,000,000 households nationally and internationally. Their World Finals is held in Las Vegas, Nevada, and they have become major players in the world of rodeo, albeit in a very specialized part.

ABOVE: Three youngsters sitting on the chutes, getting ready for their own events. Rodeo participation starts at a very early age all over the United States. Photo courtesy of Louise L. Serpa, Tucson, Arizona.

pion bronco rider . . . who encounters the adventures of contemporary rodeo life."

Then there are always the songs of Roy Rogers and the Sons of the Pioneers, Gene Autry, and Ian Tyson, who wrote such contemporary rodeo classics as "Some Day Soon," and "Old Cheyenne," in addition to his songs about the champion bronc riders Casey Tibbs and Jerry Ambler. Chris LeDoux, who was the World Champion bareback rider in 1976, wrote and sung a wide variety of songs about his life going down the road on the rodeo trail. Paul Zarzyski, a former bronc rider and referred to by a former executive director of the ProRodeo Hall of Fame as "our original rodeo poet," brings rodeo to the public through his words. Tyson has summarized rodeo and the romantic vision of the West, probably the best, as he usually does, in these four lines from "Old Cheyenne":

> *The band would play the anthem, and*
> *The clowns fell down in jest.*
> *All the people saw again*
> *The winning of the West.*

Even a movie like *Urban Cowboy* tried to tap into the romantic myth about cowboys and the "cowboy code." Maybe the most well-known of all, however, is the international cowboy symbol, the Marlboro Man, who appeared on billboards and in print ads all over the world. And it is fun, if not downright humorous, to see the local banker, grocer, hair stylist, lawyer, and other prominent citizens dress up in their Levi's or Wranglers, shiny seldom-used cowboy boots, fringed jackets, bandanas, and hats when the rodeo comes to town. It's as if everyone wants to be a part of the action.

Romantic versions of the historic shoot-outs, cattle drives up the Old Chisholm Trail, and the building of the vast ranches by larger-than-life cattle barons like Charles Goodnight and "Shanghai" Pierce, throughout the Rocky Mountains, Great Plains, and the deserts of the Southwest are all trying to recapture what was in fact a very short-lived period. From the end of the Civil War to the beginning of the twentieth century was the West's time, although elements from that early period are still kept alive on ranches all over North America, both consciously and unconsciously. Technology has crept onto most ranches but ranching is still ranching—a cowboy chasing cows from the back of a horse.

In the early days it was the Wild West shows and the new rodeos that brought cowboy and cowgirl heroics to all of North America and eventually the world. This was later enhanced by pulp fiction writers. Periodicals like *Rough Rider Weekly* and *Wild West Weekly* regularly brought the heroics of the westerner to the rest of the country. It really didn't matter whether or not the stories were true or even came close to approaching some form of honesty in the storytelling. The stories were filled with action heroes, and the good guys always beat the bad guys. In 1902, easterner Owen Wister published *The Virginian* and the modern western with the cowboy as a heroic figure was created. The Montana cowboy, Will James, followed and wrote a number of westerns that went on to be classics. Zane Grey, another of the early writers, gained international prominence in 1912 with the publication of *Riders of the Purple Sage*. More recently Jack Schaeffer's *Shane* and *Monty Walsh* have helped to define the traditional western hero. Louis L'Amour has churned out westerns almost too numerous to count. Many of those books have been made into movies and TV specials, bringing an ever-wider audience to the genre.

The real cowboys and cowgirls have survived all the hoo-ha; they will continue to survive as long as there is a demand for cattle and there are cowboys and cowgirls to oversee the job. After all, cattle just don't seem to be able to care for themselves on their way to McDonald's, Burger King, the supermarkets, and the backyard cookouts! Most of the world loves beef. As the slogan goes, "Beef—it's what's for dinner."

On the great cattle drives to the railheads from Texas up to Kansas—and the drives that were well over 1,000

RIGHT: Former World Champion bareback rider in 1976, Chris LeDoux, on "Crazy Blaze," who was owned by Cowtown Rodeos at the 1979 National Finals Rodeo. After his career in the arena, LeDoux went on to become a successful cowboy singer. Photo by Al Long, courtesy of the Professional Rodeo Cowboys Association.

OPPOSITE: Rodeo Stock contractor Don Hight (horseback) with Clint Eastwood, working on an episode of the popular TV series *Rawhide* in 1962. Courtesy of the Professional Rodeo Cowboys Association.

miles and took months all the way to the north country of Montana and Wyoming—the cowboys were tough, a little rowdy, and proud of their accomplishments. It's been estimated that somewhere between 25,000 and 35,000 cowboys pushed nearly ten million head of cattle up the trails from Texas in the period from the Civil War to the end of the nineteenth century.

In 1869, on the Smokey Hill Trail, Deer Trail, Colorado, it's generally accepted that the beginning of rodeo took place. That was the year that cowboys from the Hash Knife, Camp Stool, and the Mill Iron outfits had been boasting about who was best at the various skills that were required on the trail, especially how they handled tough horses. Every outfit had its best man in each "event," and at Deer Trail they began to brag about their respective rough string riders—guys who could really handle a bronc. Those bronc busters, or bronc stompers, were very proud of what they could accomplish with a wild or green-broke horse, so the cowboys from each of the outfits began to bet that their man was the best. It was all pretty informal—no prizes, no trophies, and most importantly, no rules as we would know them today. There were just the cowboys at trail's end, betting on their compadres. Work had become sport for those trail-weary hands, a welcome relief after months on the dry and dusty trails, riding in all kinds of weather behind thousands of cantankerous cattle.

It is generally believed that an Englishman, Emilne Gradenshire, from the Mill Iron outfit, was that year's winner by beating out the cowboys from the other ranches. He won because he was able to ride a Hash

ABOVE: Canadian Reg Kesler was primarily known as one of the leading stock contractors, but he started his career as a contestant. Here he rides "Up and Over" at Ellensburg, Washington, in 1949. Kesler is a member of both the ProRodeo Hall of Fame and the Canadian Professional Rodeo Hall of Fame.

Knife outlaw bronc named Montana Blizzard for fifteen minutes. And to show their pride and respect for what he had accomplished, the cowboys took up a collection and bought the Englishman a new suit of clothes and gave him the title of "Champion Bronco Buster of the Plains."

Those contests at the end of the great drives became very popular with cowboys. Bronc riding and steer roping were the two events that they usually competed in because the skills needed for those events were the same skills that were actually needed for the work that they normally had to do while they were months on the trail or working on the open range. The other events we associate with rodeo today—bareback riding, steer wrestling, barrel racing, team roping, and even calf roping (now called tie-down roping) were all added later. But even

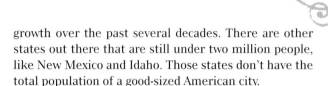

today, as a tribute to the past and in recognition of its origins and importance in the early days, saddle bronc riding is still referred to as rodeo's classic event.

By the mid- to late 1880s, the West had become a major fascination in the American psyche. Going all the way back to the period when President Thomas Jefferson dispatched Lewis and Clark (1804–1806) on their epic journey to the Pacific, the West always seemed to be the great mystery and also the escape valve for those who were, or who believed that they were, trapped in a life from which they thought they might someday want to leave. Heading out West was a real option even if it was only a psychological one. Untold films, television dramas, and stories have captured the spirit of the wagon trains, with the tough wagon boss, savvy scout, and families looking for a new life as they confronted the Indians, outlaws, and the weather on the difficult trek through the rugged western lands.

Although historians and others claimed that the frontier was officially closed in 1890 when it was estimated that there were more than two people per square mile throughout most of the region, that figure was never entirely reached in all the western states and territories, and even today there are nearly 135 counties in the West that still haven't achieved the population density of two people per square mile. In fact, there are quite a few counties that have far less than one person per square mile. There are vast areas in "cowboy country" that are still so sparsely populated (and with no real prospects of having that change over the next few decades) that often westerners have a minimum appreciation for the concept of overpopulation. Wyoming, North Dakota, South Dakota, and Montana have less than one million people in each state and they haven't experienced much growth over the past several decades. There are other states out there that are still under two million people, like New Mexico and Idaho. Those states don't have the total population of a good-sized American city.

Rodeo, the sport that grew out of an industry, was only in its infancy in the decades after the Civil War but certainly it was beginning to find its place in American culture. It is doubtful that anyone anticipated the growth that would occur over the next 150 or so years and certainly no one planned it to happen.

In an interview in *American Cowboy* magazine, the new 2005 Commissioner of the PRCA, Troy Ellerman, who is an attorney from California with a distinguished rodeo background, summarized his sport: "We have a great sport, and people love it. How often do you have three generations of a family watching an event and loving it? There's nothing phony about rodeo. It's the real deal. I truly believe it's the best sport in the world."

The Wild

West
Shows

Art Acord (1890–1951) riding "Cyclone" in 1912 in Klamath Falls, Oregon.

The Wild West shows actually preceded rodeos, and it is certainly safe to say that they set the stage for the rodeos to be successful. It's been estimated that by 1885 there were more than fifty of those extravaganzas on the road, aimed primarily at city audiences. Of all the early promoters, none made a bigger name for himself and still survives in the American imagination more than William F. Cody, our own "Buffalo Bill."

Buffalo Bill's Wild West Show ✦

Cody first appeared on stage in a show in Chicago in 1872, but it wasn't until 1886 that he created his first Wild West show and took it on the road. Many have questioned the authenticity of Cody and his shows, but despite what many cynics have said about Buffalo Bill, he was in fact the real thing—a true westerner. Of all the entrepreneurs in the early days of the shows, none was more the frontiersman, Indian scout, or western character than Cody. Paul Fees, the historian and retired curator at the Buffalo Bill Historical Center (1981–2001) in Cody, Wyoming, has written extensively about Bill Cody and some of the following is from his research.

William Frederick Cody (1846–1917) was born in a log cabin near LeClaire, Iowa Territory, on February 26, 1846. Growing up as one of eight children, Bill ("Willie" to his own family) took off on his own after he saw his father die from a fatal stabbing in 1857. He started out as a herder and mounted messenger with Russell, Majors, and Waddell—the Leavenworth, Kansas, freighting company and organizer of the Pony Express. Soon after that, he accompanied a wagon train west to Fort Laramie on the eastern plains of Wyoming.

For the next two years he trapped beaver, headed to the gold fields of Colorado, and even found time for several months of schooling. He also joined in on, "to my shame," he admitted later, some of the "border war" damage perpetrated by antislavery gangs of Jayhawkers.

After his mother died, early in 1864, he enlisted in the 7th Kansas Cavalry, a volunteer Union regiment that brought him back together with some of his old Jayhawking pals. He fought well and with honor until the end of the Civil War when he headed to St. Louis. It was there that in 1866 he met and married Louisa Frederici. It didn't take them long to pull up stakes and move to Kansas where they began what was to become a very mobile lifestyle. They had four children—Arta Lucille (1866–1904) was born in Leavenworth, Kansas; Kit Carson (1870–1876) and Orra Maude (1872–1883) were born at Fort McPherson in Nebraska; and Irma Louise (1883–1918) was born at North Platte, Nebraska.

The young Bill Cody was a lot like his father—he didn't stay home for long stretches of time. After a couple of short-lived jobs, he set out to make his life and living on the plains of the West. It was there that he became a great success at contract jobs for the army and railroad.

With his exceptional marksmanship, he was able to supply 4,280 buffalo to feed railroad construction crews during an eight-month period in 1867–68 and thus he earned his nickname, "Buffalo Bill." General Phil Sheridan thought Cody was a modest, well-spoken, natural leader and made him chief scout for the 5th Cavalry in 1868. During his several stints as a scout (1868–72, 1874, 1876), he fought in nineteen battles and skirmishes with the Indians, was wounded once, and was cited for valor and "extraordinarily good services," won the Congressional Medal of Honor for gallantry, and a month after Custer's defeat at Little Big Horn, he killed a Cheyenne leader in hand-to-hand combat and took what he called "the first scalp for Custer."

Sheridan had so much confidence and respect for Buffalo Bill that in 1872 he assigned him to guide the Grand Duke Alexis of Russia on a hunt that has been written about in numerous publications. The Russian nobleman's hunt was a major news story all over America and captured the popular imagination. One of the residual effects of the hunt was the publicity that Bill Cody received and that was extremely instrumental in launching his acting career.

Late in 1872, Cody and his buddy, Texas Jack Omohundro, himself a legendary army scout, starred in Chicago and later in New York in *The Scouts of the Prairie*, written by his friend Edward Zane Carroll Judson, who wrote thrillers and by this time had become the renowned dime novelist under the name of Ned Buntline. Buntline's writings were a major factor in how people viewed the West and westerners, particularly the romanticized and heroic images of the cowboys and Indians and Buffalo Bill. Eventually Buntline wrote nearly two hundred Buffalo Bill novels. One Chicago critic commented approvingly on the "flavor of realism and nationality" that he found in Buntline's melodrama, and it was just those qualities that came to define Cody's stage plays for the next dozen years as well as the epic that he was to become identified with more than any other event—Buffalo Bill's Wild West Show.

The Wild West Show was so well received that it lasted from 1883 until World War I. In pageants that captured the imagination of the people of his time, Cody was also able to connect America's rapid growth with "the winning of the West." These romanticized versions of the West were very easy to understand, exciting, and the message was unmistakable as he presented his extravaganza to millions of people in the United States and abroad. Cody wanted to portray life in the way that he thought the "real West" was, so he hired cowboys, Indians to re-create war dances, Mexican vaqueros, expert ropers, as well as authentic stagecoaches and emigrant wagons, together with bucking horses and a herd of buffalo. He did all of this so he could give a realistic portrayal of what he wanted the public to see of the wild life on the plains. Buffalo hunts, Pony Express riders, and an attack on the Deadwood stagecoach were all part of the show that ended with the stirring finale of "Custer's Last Stand."

At the beginning, women didn't play a major role in Cody's shows. In fact, he originally hired actresses to portray the women of the frontier. It wasn't until he signed up sharp shooters Annie Oakley and later Lillian Smith that he began to realize that the true women of the West were a big hit with the audiences. Soon after, he added twelve authentic lady riders to the cast. Women had found their place in the depiction of the American West and went on to make the most of it. To this day, Buffalo Bill—because of his touring shows and all the excitement they generated—is still one of the most recognizable Americans, especially in Europe.

Bill Cody launched his first Wild West Show on May 19, 1883, at Omaha, Nebraska. In his first season his partner was Dr. W. F. Carver, a dentist and an exhibition shooter. Their show, subtitled "Rocky Mountain and Prairie Exhibition" was wildly received across the country by both the audiences and even the critics. That was the beginning of a genre of entertainment that prospered for nearly sixty years. The irony of Cody's show is that in 1882–83 the Apaches of Arizona and New Mexico rebelled against reservation life and went on the warpath, requiring General George Crook, an experienced Indian fighter, to stop them. The Apaches were led by Geronimo and they did eventually return to the reservation. There was still real life left in the "old West," beyond that depicted in the Wild West shows.

Cody's legacy was a very dramatic image of the Wild West that has intrigued the world ever since

and made the American cowboy one of the nation's most identifiable figures. Cody remained a showman almost until his death in Denver, on January 10, 1917. More than 250,000 people filed past his remains and President Theodore Roosevelt called him "one of those men, steel-hewed and iron-nerved, whose daring progress opened the great West to settlement and civilization."

But as Paul Fees points out, the idea of a kind of exhibition like the Wild West show had been around for a long time. It certainly wasn't entirely the invention of Buffalo Bill. Fees traces it all the way back to mid-sixteenth-century France when fifty Brazilian Indians were brought to Rouen to populate a replica of their village. Elevated walkways enabled the royal spectators to watch the Indians reenact their lives back in the Amazon. In this same vein, when the Americans were developing their own presentations, American Indian life became a fixture in the Wild West shows, especially after the "wild" frontier was considered closed and the Indians had been relegated to reservations.

Even the artist George Catlin had earlier expressed his concern that if he didn't accurately capture his Indian subjects and their culture on canvas, they would be lost forever. It was his belief—and a belief he shared with many others—that the day of the Indians as they functioned in their own traditional culture was over, overrun by the invasion of European culture and society. He was so concerned that he vowed "nothing short of the loss of my life shall prevent me from visiting their country and becoming their historian."

Cody's show proved to be such a great success that in its first year it even performed at New York's Madison Square Garden, the same arena that was to become

LEFT: William F. Cody, known as "Buffalo Bill," helped define the American western frontier and produced the world famous Wild West shows. Courtesy of Zon International Publishing.

It wasn't until he signed up sharp shooters Annie Oakley and later Lillian Smith that he began to realize that the true women of the West were a big hit with the audiences.

Dorothy Morrell is winning first money in the bronc riding at Clayton, New Mexico, in 1915. An early photographer is in the foreground.

DOROTHY MORRELL WINNING FIRST MONEY CLA

Valerius Geist in his book, *Buffalo Nation*, quotes a London newspaper's review of Cody's show in 1887 for Queen Victoria's Jubilee that included Annie Oakley and Sitting Bull:

> As we took our places in one of the little boxes which edge the arena grounds of the American Exhibition where Buffalo Bill's Wild West Show is given, we could not help being struck with the effectiveness of the scene before us. There were various tribes of Indians in their war-paint and feathers, the Mexicans, the ladies, and the cowboys, and a fine array they made, with the chiefs of each tribe, and the celebrated Buffalo Bill....The buffalo hunt was immensely realistic.... Summing up the Wild West Show, we would suggest for consideration the advantage of the introduction of a little scalping. Why should not the Indians overcome a party of scouts, and 'raise their hair'?

home to the world-famous Madison Square Garden Rodeo. That rodeo, in New York, became one of the nation's major professional rodeo stops for many years. The 101 Ranch Show was another one of the touring extravaganzas to play Madison Square Garden, starting in 1905. New Yorkers, together with the rest of America, couldn't get enough of those staged reenactments of the West and how they represented life on the frontier.

The year before Cody began his Wild West shows, he produced something called the "Old Glory Blowout" in his hometown of North Platte, Nebraska, on July 4, 1882. The show had roping, buffalo riding, horsemanship, and the more traditional bronc riding and steer roping. And though he expected to attract about a hundred competitors, he and the other sponsors were amazed when they actually wound up with a thousand cowboys. That exhibition was not like his Wild West Shows that were to follow. In North Platte he offered cash prizes and that alone was enough to set a pattern for future contests. It would be hard to argue that North Platte wasn't a rodeo in the truest sense despite the fact that it still didn't quite resemble rodeos as we know them today. But surely the framework for modern-day rodeos was being put into place.

101 Ranch Wild West Show ✦ There were other shows springing up all over the country, some starring the biggest names in the western world and entertainment. In 1913, Zack Miller, together with his two brothers, Joseph and George, started the 101 Ranch Wild West Show, touring throughout North and South America. The show was so successful that they were able to stay on the road with their stage spectacular until the 1930s. Taking a different approach than Buffalo Bill, the three Miller brothers used their own ranch hands for their talent. They built their show around performances of roping, shooting, and trick riding. Almost all of the performers—among them Tom Mix, Buck Jones, and Mabel Norman, who all became silent film stars—rotated their time between the ranch and the road. The great bulldogging (now known as steer wrestling) innovator, the black cowboy Bill Pickett, traveled with the 101 until his death; he died while breaking a colt at the 101 Ranch near Ponca City, Oklahoma, in 1932, a year after the show had closed. The green-broke colt reared and kicked Pickett in the head, causing a concussion. He died eleven days

Even at this early stage in the nation's move west, Americans wanted heroes and were already nostalgic as they sensed the end of the frontier and all the freedoms that it implied.

later at the age of sixty-one and was buried on the 101 Ranch in Oklahoma.

Pickett was born near Austin, Texas, the son of freed slaves, something not uncommon in the growing West. By the time he was a teenager he was making some money by breaking horses and giving demonstrations of what was to become his trademark—wrestling steers. Pickett developed all of his ranch skills and was once described by a Wild West Show director as "the greatest sweat and dirt cowhand that ever lived—bar none." The story goes that Pickett, in 1908, while wrestling down a steer, bit the critter's lip. Supposedly his boss called attention to the fact that Pickett was a regular "bulldog," the way he held onto the steer with his teeth.

Bulldogging and Pickett became so popular that in 1923, Hollywood produced a silent film called *The Bull-Dogger*, featuring an all-black cast with Bill Pickett as the star. Because of segregation at that time, the film unfortunately played only in black movie theaters and had a very small audience.

Initially, bulldogging was not as much of a competitive event as it was an exhibition at the Wild West shows. It was some years later before steer wrestling was actually established as part of the competition for the cowboys at the Pendleton Round-Up. That was 1911 and it proved to be so popular that other rodeos soon adopted it as part of their own program. Nowadays you don't see cowboys biting the lip of a steer, but you do see them wrestling some pretty stout steers using great strength and athletic ability.

Setting the Stage for Rodeo ✦ The Wild West shows' popularity continued to grow because they featured not only the pageantry of the West but also the skills of both the cowboys and the cowgirls. Even at this early stage in the nation's move West, Americans wanted heroes and were already nostalgic as they sensed the end of the frontier and all the freedoms that it implied. America, together with the rest of the world, was entering into the industrial age, and even at this early stage there was a yearning for a return to the frontier west. In 1895, for example, Buffalo Bill's Wild West Show played in 131 cities.

Although the Wild West shows were not contests in the true sense of the word—all the participants were on contract and not actually competing for prize money—it did set the stage for the early rodeos where a contestant had to either win or at least place in order to take home a paycheck.

THE NORMAN FILM MFG. CO.
PRESENTS

BILL PICKETT
WORLD'S COLORED CHAMPION—IN
'THE BULL-DOGGER'
Featuring The Colored Hero of the Mexican Bull Ring in Death Defying Feats of Courage and Skill.
THRILLS! LAUGHS TOO!
Produced by NORMAN FILM MFG. CO.
JACKSONVILLE, FLA.

RIGHT: A poster from the Buffalo Bill/Pawnee Bill Wild West Shows from around 1910. Women were frequently featured on these posters. Courtesy of Zon International Publishing.

The Beginning of Real

Rodeo

Black cowboy George Fletcher fanning "Hot Foot" with his hat in Pendleton, 1911.

As the country became more and more populated, particularly in the West, the new and growing communities (as well as the older ones) held celebrations—to commemorate their founding, the coming of the railroad, the Fourth of July, or some other patriotic event. Very often they began to hold rodeos as part of these celebrations, with the local cowboys demonstrating their skills for their neighbors.

Occasionally cowboys came from out of the immediate area just to prove their superiority in face-to-face competition with the locals. These were not professional rodeo cowboys; they were working ranch hands. The skills used in the competitive events at these celebrations were actually the same skills that the cowboys needed as part of their daily chores. Yet as time moved forward, ranching changed, and the country got further and further away from its frontier origins, these events became a reliving of the past. The Wild West shows and dime novels continued to exaggerate and romanticize the latter part of the nineteenth century in the West. Cowboy culture was, for all intents and purposes, well established in the American psyche and folklore, and rodeo was becoming a fixture of both the recreational and professional sports scenes all over the country.

Rodeos began to spring up in every part of the West—in Pecos, Texas, for example, on July 4, 1883, with cowboys from the Hash Knife, W, Lazy Y, and NA ranches competing in bronc riding and steer roping before nearly 1,000 spectators. There was no admission—the "arena" was an open field near the courthouse—and local ranchers put up $40 for the winner of the bronc riding, a cowboy whose name has been lost to history.

For the steer roping, the animals were just set free to run down the main street of Pecos with the ropers after them. Trav Windham, a Texas cowboy, was the winner of the contest that day. He took home a small winner's purse and a blue ribbon made from the trim of a young girl's dress. This event developed into the West of the Pecos Rodeo, a rodeo the cowboys still consider a pretty good stop. Today, in the town of barely 9,500 people, the local businesses still manage to raise over $200,000 in prize money, placing it among the top thirty rodeos on the professional circuit. Soon after the 1883 event, localized contests like the one in Pecos began to spring up in small- and medium-size towns and eventually in cities throughout the old frontier.

There are rodeo historians who claim that way back in 1844, before the Civil War, before cowboys and cowgirls, before the whole concept of western ranching had become widespread, Major Jack Hays of the Texas Rangers organized a competition in San Antonio that pitted his Rangers, Comanche warriors, and Mexican vaqueros against one another in riding and shooting contests. If you really want to go back in time, you could probably make a pretty good case that rodeo actually started with the old Mexican *charreria* tradition, which is a series of events held at a *charreada*, which is the Mexican rodeo. The *charro* usually learns his skills from his father and they are passed on from generation to generation.

As far back as 1537 there were so many stray cattle and wild horses in New Spain that the Spanish authorities required ranchers to brand and castrate their livestock each year at a roundup that came to be known as the "rodeo del Ganado." Certainly the influence of the vaqueros on the future North American cowboys can't be overstated. The traditions and sharing of cultures continued until the post–Civil War period in the United States. Even today, so much of the cowboy's gear, culture, and even language have been derived from his vaquero amigos. Even the term *buckaroo* is a variation of the word *vaquero*. There is no doubt that the Mexican vaqueros taught the Americans how to be cowboys.

One year after Pecos, in 1884, the town of Payson, Arizona, had a bronc riding contest. Albuquerque, New Mexico, in 1886, held a fair with the winning steer roper receiving a new saddle. In 1887, at the Colorado Exposition in Denver, admission to a rodeo was charged for the first time and over 12,000 people showed up to cheer on the cowboys.

Prescott, Arizona

By 1888, Prescott, Arizona, formed a committee of local merchants, including Morris Goldwater (Barry Goldwater's uncle), to organize a rodeo. The committee also made sure that good cowboys participated and charged spectators an admission fee. The contestants were awarded prizes and the rodeo has continued in that town each year since. In July, at that first rodeo, steer roping was the main event. Juan Levias, a Mexican-American cowboy from the James O'Neal Ranch on Date Creek in Arizona, was awarded the first medal, the Citizen's Prize, for roping a steer that had been given a 100-yard start. His time was 1 minute and 17.5 seconds. Levias also tied for first with Charlie Meadows in bronc riding. The next year Levias entered again, winning the bronc riding contest and placing second to Jeff Young in steer roping. That same year the committee added steer riding, and it became a very popular event. Tom Mix won that event in 1913. In 1914, Prescott, Arizona, added bareback riding, which was won by a cowboy named Doc Pardee. Calf roping was added in 1917 and won by H. Eubank. In 1919, team roping became a regular part of the celebration.

And it was from that beginning that Prescott got to be known as "The Roping Capital of the World," although the rodeo's modern name—Prescott Frontier Days—wasn't adopted until 1913, the first year the rodeo was held on the Yavapai County Fairgrounds.

Cheyenne, Wyoming

In 1891, a cowboy competition was held in Miles City, Montana. The cowboys were there to entertain the members of the Montana Stock Growers Association and they contested only for trophies, no money.

ABOVE: The Wild Horse Race, Prescott, Arizona, 1984. Photo courtesy of Louise L. Serpa, Tucson, Arizona.

The 1893 Frontier Days at Lander, Wyoming, claims to be the first contest that was strictly a commercial rodeo. It wasn't part of any civic or patriotic event—it was just a rodeo staged by E. Farlow, who added a ten-mile, three-horse team relay race and a stagecoach holdup to the regular rodeo events. In 1896, the cow town of Mingersville, now known as Wibaux, out on the eastern plains of Montana, held a small rodeo.

But one year after Mingersville, in 1897, Cheyenne, Wyoming, held its first Frontier Days, and it claims to be the oldest continuous cowboy contest on record, although Prescott doesn't necessarily agree. By all accounts the Arizona city actually owns the title "The World's Oldest Rodeo." Prescott has held its rodeo every year since 1888 without a break. No other rodeo can claim a longer unbroken run. Cheyenne is now called "The Daddy of Them All," a title that aptly describes the prestige and place Cheyenne holds in the rodeo world. Cheyenne probably is the Big Daddy. Their rodeo has the most contestants and the biggest arena—so big that part of it has had to be fenced off to accommodate the ropers and give the arena people some control over the bucking stock. Cheyenne has the biggest rodeo grounds and the most prize money of any regular season rodeo, and it is second overall to any rodeo except for the Wrangler National Finals. Cheyenne's purse now exceeds $840,000. To top that off, in these days of easy travel, they draw about 400,000 people to the nine performances held the last full week in July, the largest crowd in rodeo.

Like many of those early rodeos, though, their origins are fairly inauspicious. In Cheyenne a few businessmen were returning from Greeley, Colorado's "Potato Day," when Colonel E. A. Slack, owner and editor of the *Cheyenne Daily Sun*, came to the realization that Cheyenne should have its own festival rather than go to their neighbor's to the south. Besides, the country

Cheyenne has the biggest rodeo grounds and the most prize money of any regular season rodeo, and it is second overall to any rodeo except for the Wrangler National Finals.

around Cheyenne was hardly farm country. It was high-plains desert, good grazing land trying to recover from the disastrous winter of 1886–87. Slack, along with Frederick W. Angier, a Traveling Passenger Agent for the Union Pacific Railroad, put a committee together with the help of the newly elected mayor, William M. Schnitger. In twenty-three days the trio organized and staged their first Frontier Days.

The railroad had been urging all the towns along the rail line to hold a festival or a fair, in order to become a destination for an excursion train. Cheyenne needed the event to help rebuild the city and area economies. The initial celebration had six horse races, a pitching and bucking horse contest, and a steer-roping contest. Surprisingly, the crowds came to Cheyenne that first year, in part because the festivities were advertised throughout the United States and the Union Pacific ran special trains to bring people to the Wyoming capital. (Far and away the most popular train was the Union Pacific excursion train from Denver that even had a band on board to entertain the passengers.) At the fairgrounds where the rodeo was held, it was standing room only. Shirley Flynn, in her history of Frontier Days, describes the celebration at the rodeo grounds: "The overflow crowd packed in around the track either standing on the ground or seated in conveyances. Most people carried umbrellas for protection from possible rain or the sun. Whenever a steer or bucking horse came toward the fence, umbrellas were immediately raised and pointed toward the animal to turn him away." Flynn explains that no admission was charged to the grounds, bleacher seats were 15 cents, grandstand seats were 35 cents, and the entire space around the half-mile track was packed five to ten people deep. One reporter, bursting with civic pride, guessed the crowd was around 15,000, but Flynn estimates that a more realistic number would have been 4,000.

By 1898 the Frontier Days rodeo lasted two full days, and for the first time the Shoshone Indians from the Fort Washakie Reservation in central Wyoming were invited to perform dances and to take part in a simulated attack on a wagon train. Various Indian nations have been participating at Cheyenne ever since and there is now a full-scale Indian Village on the grounds.

RIGHT: Part of the official program for Cheyenne Frontier Days in 1938. Photo courtesy of the Professional Rodeo Cowboys Association.

Cheyenne has always had a special place in the popular imagination and has therefore always attracted interesting and famous people. In 1898, Buffalo Bill's Wild West Show performed in Cheyenne before a cheering crowd of 6,000, causing George Eastman of Kodak to comment, "We should have a moving picture of this." In 1903, President Theodore Roosevelt passed through town late in May, and the town made sure that a special rodeo was performed for him. Roosevelt requested that only cowboy contests be held and he couldn't get enough of the roping and bronc riding. And even though the events for Roosevelt were held on a Monday, the stands were crowded and the president seemed to love every minute of it.

In 1906, Cheyenne added ladies' bronc riding as a regular contest and amateur bronc riding, a contest for rookie cowboys that became a permanent event in 1911.

Another distinction for Cheyenne is that in 1920 they added calf roping, won that year by Fred Beeson, and then

One of the fastest-growing competitions is the ranch rodeo, for working cowhands, where a group of cowboys and cowgirls represent their particular ranch rather than themselves.

in 1936 they crowned their first champion in bareback riding, Chuck Hanson, and in bull riding, Shorty Hill. These last two contests became regular events; Cheyenne was one of the first rodeos to hold them as part of their regular schedule although the first World Champion bareback rider was crowned in 1932. Bull riding had been contested at both Prescott and Calgary for at least a decade before it became a permanent event at Cheyenne.

McCarty and Elliott ✦ Bull riding posed serious problems unlike any for the other events. In addition to occasionally being uncontrollable, the bulls often did not buck. Two stock contractors, Ed McCarty and Verne Elliott, developed a crossbred critter, using Brahma cattle from India. Rodeo was changed forever because of those early crosses with the cattle from India, and for many years bull riding was known to both the cowboys and the public as "Brahma bull riding."

Both McCarty and Elliott were well known in the rodeo world and had, in 1917, produced the first indoor rodeo ever staged. It was at Fort Worth, Texas, and the next year they produced the first Madison Square Garden rodeo. Elliott was also one of the first rodeo producers to take the sport to England. The event took place in 1924 and was a big success. In a ceremony in Arizona in 1936, Verne Elliott was initiated into the Navajo Nation and given the name of Acalthe Binantai, which in English translates to "Mr. Head Cowboy." The Navajos got that right!

Ed McCarty grew up in Cheyenne and saw one of the first frontier shows in 1900, when contestants brought in their own bucking horses. McCarty became a contestant and a good one. He won the steer roping contest in 1909, the year he graduated from Cheyenne High School, and then went on to win the bulldogging contest in 1914 and the saddle bronc riding contest in 1919.

Together, Elliott and McCarty, in the 1930s and 1940s, owned two of the greatest bucking horses of all time, "Midnight" and "Five Minutes to Midnight." Both horses were inducted into the ProRodeo Hall of Fame in 1979, along with "Hell's Angel," who in 1940 was voted as the "greatest bucker of all time." This horse was originally owned by Colonel W. T. Johnson and when he sold out in

1937, the horse wound up in the string of Everett Colborn. One night, coming back from a rodeo, "Hell's Angel" was found dead in her railroad car when the train stopped in Poplar Bluff, Missouri. They buried her there.

Pendleton, Oregon

The Pendleton, Oregon, Round-Up began as a full-fledged rodeo in 1910 and to this day is still considered one of the most prestigious and colorful of all the rodeos on the circuit. The year before, in 1909, they had held a two-day bronc-riding competition as part of the Eastern Oregon District Fair. The first day's winner was a teenager named Lee "Babe" Caldwell, who took home a $45 Hamley-McFarridge saddle. A rancher named Herbert Thompson took second and the $25 prize, and a black cowboy, George Fletcher, took third and earned $15. Caldwell, just sixteen at the time of his triumph at Pendleton, later became one of the most celebrated bronc busters of his era, winning not only at Pendleton but at Cheyenne, Calgary, and many of the other new contests being held throughout North America.

The second day at Pendleton, C. S. Tipton, a horse breaker from Walla Walla, won the event, and his prize was a hand-carved saddle from the E. L. Powers harness store. Guy Hayes took second, and another young cowboy, Del Blancett, took the third prize of $15. This event was so successful that by the next year the local businessmen had created the Pendleton Round-Up. Virgil Rupp in his 1985 history of the Pendleton Round-Up reports that the aim of the new event was to be a "frontier exhibition of picturesque pastimes, Indian and military spectacles, cowboy racing and bronco busting." This all sounds as much like a Wild West show as it does a rodeo, but Pendleton, now one of the premier rodeos on the national circuit, had begun.

In 1910, Pendleton had seven bronc riders competing for a $300 purse, won by John Fredericks. In 1911 steer wrestling, or bulldogging, was acknowledged as a true rodeo event, and Pendleton put together the first rules for the competition and created a cash purse for the winner, a cowboy named Buffalo Vernon.

Pendleton almost collapsed under the weight of its own success. In 1911, on the first day of the three-day show, 12,000 people showed up. On Saturday, 15,000 watched the championships, including the legendary bronc-riding contest between Jackson Sundown (a Nez Perce Indian), George Fletcher (a well-known black cowboy), and John Spain (a member of a local ranching family). When the competition ended and Spain was declared

Both McCarty and Elliott were well known in the rodeo world and had, in 1917, produced the first indoor rodeo ever staged.

Ed McCarty, the stock contractor, riding one of his own saddle broncs, "Last Chance," at a Cheyenne rodeo in 1910. Photo courtesy of the Professional Rodeo Cowboys Association.

the winner with Fletcher second, "the crowd moaned," according to Virgil Rupp. He adds, "Newspaper accounts say that although Fletcher easily made the most showy ride to the average spectator, the judges, all experienced stockman, had a different perspective. They ruled that

ABOVE: A team roping taking place in Moe, Victoria, in Australia, 1972. Courtesy of the Professional Rodeo Cowboys Association.

Spain's form was better and that he had a much harder mount to handle." Rodeo historians and fans love to discuss that contest to this day, and the possibility of local racism often becomes part of the discussion. Was a black cowboy or an Indian cowboy going to be judged superior to a white cowboy? Times were different in 1911.

The Oregon rodeo always seems to have had more than its share of fascinating characters. The three riders in the famous bronc contest of 1911 were all extraordinary cowboys. One of the most popular bronc riders from the early days was Jackson Sundown, a Nez Perce Indian cowboy from Cul-de-sac, Idaho, and a nephew of the legendary Chief Joseph. He was the first full-blooded Indian to ever win a major rodeo championship. George Fletcher was known for riding the meanest outlaw horses "as though he was in a ballroom" and for riding bucking horses backward, a feat that got him injured every now and again. John Spain, born in 1881 at Cottage Grove, in eastern Oregon, won the saddle bronc championship in 1911. After that he lost a hand in a roping accident, but in the true spirit of "cowboying up," he continued to rodeo and continued to win. Spain, together with his brother Fred, was asked by the director of livestock operations at Pendleton, Til Taylor, to supply bucking horses for the first Round-Up, so Fred and John trailed a herd of bucking horses eighty-five miles to be ready for the rodeo.

John's nephew recalls in an interview that he gave to Doug and Cathy Jory for their insightful oral history of rodeo, *From Pendleton to Calgary*, that when the

"When the cowboy shows up at the Round-Up and goes before a packed grandstand of 35,000 people, he wants a horse that no one else can ride."

Spain brothers were young men they were raised in a country that was teeming with wild horses. "About all they did was chase them damn wild horses an' catch an' break 'em. They'd sell 'em to the cavalry. Fred and John made a drive in 1902 with two other fellows. They made the drive from Malheur to almost the Canadian border. There was a remount station there. They took 600 head of horses up there. . . . They were old time cowboys, the real article. They either rode or had to walk, an' they didn't like walkin'." John died at the age of forty-seven from a non-rodeo injury—bleeding ulcers that went unattended.

Pendleton always had a reputation for putting on a wild and exciting show. In another interview for the Jory book, Wayne Davis, who won the "World" at Pendleton in saddle bronc riding in 1938, recalls, "They didn't play music between rides. . . . They always had something else going on—an Indian race, or relay race, or a pack-saddle race, or an Indian girl's race."

On the ladies' side, Prairie Rose Henderson took on the cowboys. Cowgirls were an important part of the early rodeos, a carryover from the Wild West Shows. Prairie Rose was the first cowgirl in Pendleton to compete in bronc riding and finished just a few points behind the winner. Ruth Roach, another one of the cowgirls from early rodeos, was known for her heart-embossed boots and satin bloomers. She was also known as a heck of a bronc rider, even winning at Fort Worth in 1917. Another female star was Kitty Canutt, whose husband was the great cowboy, and later Hollywood stuntman, actor, and second unit director, Yakima Canutt. Kitty was the All-Around Champion Cowgirl at the 1916 Round-Up.

As the Pendleton rodeo grew, the committee was gathering up some of the meanest, wildest outlaw horses for the bucking horse contest. From the beginning Pendleton was determined to put together its own bucking horse string. Rupp reports that an account of

the day said that what they wanted was "not the ordinary bucking horses who will hop, skip and jump all over a 40-acre field, but the outlaw who will throw his rider in less than 30 seconds or not at all." Another writer described it best: "When the cowboy shows up at the Round-Up and goes before a packed grandstand of 35,000 people, he wants a horse that no one else can ride."

Just before the Round-Up each year, the rodeo committee offered to pay cowboys $2.50 for each horse they would get on to see if the horse was a real bucker. Those that didn't fire out were removed from the bucking string. The sum of $2.50 might not seem like a great deal of money but to get an idea of what rodeo prices were like for the public, a fee of $1.50 was established for a box seat, $1 for the grandstand, 75 cents for the bleachers, and 50 cents for all of those who came on horseback and for children under twelve years of age. Even the budget for the first Round-Up was modest, at least by today's standards. That first year's expenses were $2,860, and by 1990 that sum had grown to $713,000. Later on it was at Pendleton that the title "Champion All-Around Cowboy" was first awarded.

Canadian Rodeo ✦ In 1912, rodeo really went beyond the borders of the United States when Guy Weadick started the Calgary Stampede in Canada. That was not Canada's first rodeo though. The credit for that goes back to 1902 at the Raymond Stampede in Raymond, Alberta, organized by Ray Knight. Knight was instrumental in establishing the Canadian tradition of always having the best bucking stock at their rodeos. There is also pretty good documentation from the *Calgary Weekly Herald* of a series of cowboy contests held at the midsummer fair in Calgary as early as 1893. Clifford P. Westermeier, in his definitive book on early rodeo, *Man, Beast, Dust*, has a fairly complete account of the early days of rodeo in Canada.

But the big push for Canadian rodeo does belong to Calgary, although some years later than the earlier events of 1893. In 1911, two Americans, Guy Weadick, along with his partner, the future movie cowboy Tom Mix (both refugees from the Miller Brothers 101 Ranch Wild West

Show) tried to get the show off the ground but weren't quite able to obtain the organization and money to pull it off. By the next year, 1912, Mix had returned to the United States, while Weadick decided to stay in Canada and continue to try to start the rodeo that he wanted.

Guy "Cheyenne Bill" Weadick was born in Rochester, New York, in 1885 and because he never seemed interested in the family tradition of law, he left the East at fourteen and worked as a cowboy from border to border—from Montana down to New Mexico. In 1904, he

went to Calgary with Bill Pickett to buy some horses, and while they were there they put on a small rodeo. Weadick had appeared in the Miller Brothers 101 Wild West Show with his wife, Florence La Due, as "Weadick & La Due Lariat Experts," and had the reputation as "the fastest roping act in vaudeville." He left the Millers in 1908, to return and then leave again.

In Canada, Weadick was eventually able to persuade several local ranchers—the "Big 4" of Pat Burns, George Lane, A. E. Cross, and A. J. McLean—to put up a total of $100,000, an enormous amount of money at that time, to establish the Calgary Stampede. It had far and away the richest purse in the rodeo world. With that kind of money, they could draw the best cowboys and cowgirls. Weadick put up a total of $20,000 in gold for the rodeo with a guarantee of $1,000 for each first-place winner in the major events. Tom Three Persons, from the Blood Reserve at Cardston, Alberta, rode the great bucking horse "Cyclone" in the finals and won the $1,000 prize

ABOVE: Action in the arena during the Wild Horse Race in London, England, 1920s. Don Nesbitt is about to pick up his saddle. Photo courtesy of the Professional Rodeo Cowboys Association.

RIGHT: The Elliott/Nesbitt rodeo stock on railroad cars heading to the rodeo grounds from the boat in London, England, 1924. This was for the rodeo put on for the Queen of England. Photo courtesy of the Professional Rodeo Cowboys Association.

Rodeo Bullfighters ✦ The 1920s were an innovative time for rodeo. Homer Holcomb of Idaho was one of the first rodeo clowns to actually "fight" a bull. Today the rodeo bullfighters are some of the most respected people in all of rodeo. The idea of the rodeo clown doing comedy acts, which for years was a staple of most rodeos, has partially given way to the more serious work of the bullfighters, especially as the bulls get bigger, tougher, and meaner. Joe Baumgartner (the 2005 Bullfighter of the Year), Darrell Diefenbach, Rob Smets, Frank Newsom, Flint Rasmussen, Barry Rowdy, Joe Brogan, Jeff Franks, and the Canadians T. J. Baird and Scott Byrne, are just a very few of the men who risk serious injury at each performance and are without doubt, the bull rider's best friend.

OPPOSITE: Wacey Cathy winning the $50,000 bonus with a 92-point ride aboard Girletz Rodeo Stock's bull "O 13 Blaster" at the 1990 Calgary Stampede. Photo by Ray Johnson, courtesy of the Professional Rodeo Cowboys Association.

plus a saddle and a gold buckle. Harry Webb of Wyoming won $500 and Charles McKinley of California won $250 for coming in second and third in what everyone considered a very exciting beginning for Calgary.

For the women, the bucking horse competition proved to be every bit as thrilling as it was for the men. With less than one point separating the top three lady bronc riders, Montana's Fanny Sperry Steele took first, Goldie Sinclair of Oklahoma came in second, and Bertha Blancett of Colorado took third. They took home the same prize money as the men.

Everyone seemed to agree that one of the most explosive events at Calgary that year was the cowgirl's relay race, because of the Canadian entry Mrs. H. McKenzie of Crossfield, Alberta. Mrs. McKenzie and the American, Bertha Blancett, waged a bitter battle with Blancett finally winning. Fanny Sperry Steele came in third.

Fourteen thousand people were in the stands for the opening performance and although the rodeo dragged on for hours, the crowd seemed to love it. Despite terrible weather the second day, the crowd still numbered thirteen thousand.

New York City ✦ Rodeo was becoming a new and popular sport with increasingly large purses. The next year, in 1913, Weadick branched out and offered another $20,000 in prize money at Winnipeg and then topped that in 1916 by putting up $50,000 in his promotion of a New York Stampede in Brooklyn's Sheepshead Bay, not too far from Coney Island. A polio epidemic and a citywide subway strike that year almost bankrupted him. The crowds just didn't show up. But it wasn't all bad news. The spectators who did make it out to the rodeo grounds were in awe of what they saw, and the press treated it to banner headlines, making it much easier for future rodeo promoters to get a foothold in the New York market.

In the early days of rodeo, the awarding of prize money and the total purses were not very consistent.

RIGHT: Jimmy Dix of North Collie, W. Australia, was one of the first of the many Australians to come and compete in North America. A multiple NFR contestant, here Dix is riding Brookman Rodeo Company's "Slick Rock" at the 1977 NFR. Photo courtesy of the Professional Rodeo Cowboys Association.

While Weadick was raising $100,000 in Calgary and changing the financial structure of rodeo, it was just a few years earlier, on September 23, 1897, a cowboy by the name of William Jones who had come up the trail on a cattle drive from Texas won the bronc riding contest at Cheyenne and took home the meager sum of $25. His mount, the bucking horse that carried him to the championship, a bronc named "Warrior," was owned by Nelson Perry of LaGrange and took home $100 for being named the best bucking horse at the show. Fred Bath, William Cramer, and Thad Sowder, all Wyoming cowboys, won the bronc riding contest in the years following William Jones, and their winnings never came close to what was going to be offered in Calgary.

Clifford Westermeier points out that just a few years later, rodeo was getting a foothold in Australia, where the first rodeo was held in 1929. "It was given considerable publicity and was the first rodeo to be broadcast throughout the continent. It was successful, both from the standpoint of finances and entertainment, and from a radius of hundreds of miles came many people who camped in their cars near the contest grounds." By the 1960s, Australian cowboys, with bareback rider Jimmy Dix leading the way, were coming to the United States and Canada and making a big impact, particularly in the rough stock events.

In the 1920s, another dynamic early promoter entered the picture. After Guy Weadick got into financial trouble, John Van "Tex" Austin decided to try New York. He proved to be so successful that the idea that rodeo was a sport that could be enjoyed only by westerners was put to rest once and for all. In 1922, Austin put on a twenty-performance rodeo at Madison Square Garden that had the audiences going wild. One New York newspaper wrote: "Tex Austin has punctured a belief widely held that spectators for a rodeo had to be drawn from people more or less indigenous to the western cattle country. That is all bunk. New York is full of enthusiasts. At the Garden they stand in their seats and yell themselves hoarse. They behave like crazy folk."

Tex Austin was a westerner, born on a cattle ranch near Victoria, Texas, in 1887. Following a stint in

RIGHT: Terry Etzkorn bursting out of the chutes on Korkow-Sutton's "Brown Jug" at Mobridge, South Dakota, in 1969. Photo by Rathbun Rodeo Photos, courtesy of the Professional Rodeo Cowboys Association.

LEFT: Jeff Kozba, a bullfighter from Claypool, Arizona, at work at the Yuma, Arizona, rodeo in 1983. Note the fallen rider behind the bull's right hind quarters. Photo courtesy of Louise L. Serpa, Tucson, Arizona.

Mexico where he worked alongside the native vaqueros, he joined other American cowboys in the Mexican Revolution that in 1911 ousted President Diaz. After he returned to the United States, he bought the Forked Lightening Ranch near Las Vegas, New Mexico, and lived there until his death in 1941. Throughout his career he always had a good understanding of the cowboys and the work they were doing, and his shows, whether they were in New York, Boston, Chicago, London, or Hollywood, featured the best stock and the best cowboys.

In 1923, Austin brought an even bigger rodeo to New York's hallowed Yankee Stadium and then had six more successes between 1925 and 1930 in Chicago. Rodeo was actually going to the big eastern and mid-western cities and winning fans. Austin also shares the credit, along with Verne Elliott of Wyoming, for introducing the real rodeo—not the Wild West shows—to England in 1924. Austin brought his rodeo to Wembley as part of the British Empire Exposition, where he broke all existing attendance records. The rodeo was known as the First International Rodeo or Cowboy Championships.

Animal Welfare ✦ Austin did, however, get into some trouble with the Royal Humane Society because of what they perceived as cruel treatment of animals, particularly in the calf-roping and steer-roping contests. In 1934, he brought another rodeo to England and again ran into trouble with the Royal Humane Society. Tex Austin was arrested for cruelty to animals but after all sorts of legal maneuvering, the case was settled when the British authorities agreed not to prosecute him if Austin would eliminate calf roping from the rodeo. Austin agreed and the four-week show went on without anymore trouble.

For awhile, confrontations with animal rights groups were ongoing, not only in England but also in the United States and Canada. Over the years the various rodeo associations have been very conscious of their responsibilities and created a policy that is in place today. The PRCA states in their own media guide that they have "a long-standing commitment to the proper care and treatment of the livestock used in rodeo. As an association, the PRCA has been very proactive in establishing rules and regulations governing animal welfare and creating veterinary advisory groups to assist in the association's efforts in this important area." There is considerably less controversy about the treatment of animals at rodeos today and almost all people who do attend a professional rodeo can see for themselves the

humane treatment the animals receive—in the arena, in the chutes, and in the pens. The animals are not hidden away from the public.

In a fascinating perspective on the entire issue with the various humane associations and rodeo, Kristine Fredriksson speculates that maybe "some of the protests may have been aimed more at the cowboy himself and the unorganized, itinerant rodeos of the day. The rodeo cowboy of that time was, for example, described as a 'bum' rather than as a man engaged in legitimate professional sport. By exploiting the cruelty angle, those who did not want cowboys around were more likely to be heard, since the humane movement had already gained momentum." This is certainly an interesting approach to the subject and one that should not be rejected out of hand. There is no question that cowboys had an image problem in the early days, particularly before the formation of the Cowboys' Turtles Association in 1936.

the early rodeo competitions, there was no uniformity for the rules, even for the few rules that did exist. Each local rodeo committee interpreted them as they saw fit and the cowboys and cowgirls had no say. The rules as we know them today evolved gradually over decades. It wasn't until much later when the national associations were formed that there was a vestige of consistency in the events and that the rules began to be applied evenly from one rodeo to another.

> **It wasn't until much later when the national associations were formed that there was a vestige of consistency in the events and that the rules began to be applied evenly from one rodeo to another.**

Willard H. Porter, who knew rodeo well, wrote: "Although most of the top-echelon performers were reliable gents, this was not true (particularly in pre-Turtle days) of a great many lesser rodeo figures, hangers-on, and minglers. To some, the rodeo experience was a pastime, an excuse to party, drink, fight, and raise the old devil. There were probably as many, maybe more, unscrupulous contestants as there were promoters."

Bronc Riding and Steer Roping ✦ As the early rodeo "circuit" began to grow, it became very obvious that bronc riding and steer roping continued to be the featured events. The public liked and understood that the events and the skills required to be successful in them were the skills that the cowboys had developed since they first started working the herds after the Civil War. But in

The evolution of bronc riding from its place as part of the cowboy's job on the open range was slow but steady. Eventually it became one of the most intricate parts of rodeo, and rules had to be introduced to provide some consistency from one show to another. On the range there was no time limit for riding new broncs, and cowboys just rode until their mount stopped bucking and the cowboy could kick away his stirrups, use his spurs, and take off with the horse out onto the open prairie or flats. That was considered the best there was in bronc riding and the cowboys even had a name for it—"the balanced ride."

This same term would come to be used again and again as a way to describe some of the best and smoothest rodeo saddle bronc riders of professional rodeo. Jerry Ambler, Casey Tibbs, and Deb Copenhaver are three of the best who exemplified this style well into the modern period.

When bronc riding was moved into enclosed arenas to accommodate the more formal concept of rodeo, everyone agreed that there had to be some rules, if for no other reason than to keep the horses fresh and provide time for more riders to enter the event without each cowboy running on and on with five- and ten-minute rides. The rules started out by requiring a ten-second ride to qualify, and judges often just shot off a pistol to signal that ten seconds had elapsed and that the ride was over. It wasn't until 1912 that the front delivery of "shotgun chutes," came into use. But because they proved to be dangerous as the cowboys came out of the chutes, a side delivery chute was developed at Fort Worth in 1927, the same kind used today.

Until the creation of the chutes, the wild horses were usually snubbed to a gentler saddle horse or "eared down" by cowboys on the ground. They were blindfolded, saddled, and mounted in the arena with the blindfold pulled away as the ride began. The early rules were never very specific and not evenly applied. At the beginning it was agreed that if the rider kicked away one or both stirrups it would still be a qualified ride. By 1914, that rule was changed and it was decided that if a contestant was going to use his stirrups, he had to ride that way from start to finish. Or the opposite would apply; if the cowboy didn't start using his stirrups, he had to finish his ride that way. In the same year it was agreed that hobbled stirrups—those tied together under the belly of the horse near the cinch—were to be outlawed for the men but still be permitted for the lady bronc riders. "Pulling leather" or holding on to the saddle was also outlawed.

In 1911, a cowboy by the name of Charlie McKinley, from Platteville, Colorado, won the finals in the bronc riding contest at Cheyenne without using his stirrups.

In 1904, Harry Brannan apparently had a unique style of spurring his broncs, from the horse's neck to the cantle board of the saddle—a style of bronc riding that other cowboys adopted and that is still the basic style today. That year he won the title, World Champion Bronc Rider at Cheyenne, riding one of the all-time great bucking horses, "Steamboat." That great horse was owned by the Irwin Brothers, and when they toured with their Wild West Show, "Steamboat" was one of their main attractions.

Travel ✦ Another creative and ultimately very important contribution was made to rodeo by the Bowman brothers, Everett, Skeets, and Dick. Dick's son Lewis recounts that in 1924 rodeo saw its first horse trailer. The brothers Everett and Skeets were "en route from Safford, Arizona, to the Cheyenne Frontier Days Rodeo. . . . Their horse trailer, the first ever seen on the rodeo circuit, was made by their older brother, Dick, in a matter of a few hours. It took them the better part of a week to make this trip of some 1,000 miles; roads weren't top notch in those days, nor was their equipment. They were either stopping to patch a tire or looking for a stream to park in, to soak the wooden spokes of their wheels."

When you match the Bowman's trailer against today's modern rigs, it seems impossible that in the early days the cowboys and cowgirls were actually able to get from one rodeo to another with a horse. Trains were the transportation of the day for both the stock, the cowboys, and the stock contractors.

Times have definitely changed and the cowboys are far more mobile, particularly with air travel so accessible. In 2002, Jesse Bail, a twenty-three-year-old All-Around Cowboy from Camp Crook, South Dakota, won $33,456 during "Cowboy Christmas," the July 4th weekend, by competing in six states and two countries, traveling 17,497 miles. For all that travel he actually worked in the arena a total of three minutes, mostly in bull riding and saddle bronc riding.

LEFT: The famous Bowman horse trailer. It took the better part of a week in 1924 to make the 1,000 mile trek from Safford, Arizona, to Cheyenne in what is believed to be the first horse trailer seen on the rodeo circuit. Photo courtesy of Lewis Bowman and "Bumfuzzled."

Prairie Rose Henderson riding saddle bronc "Miss Cheyenne," c. 1925 at Cheyenne Frontier Days.

Cowgirls in

the Arena

As the idea of rodeo began to take hold, it made room for another very important element of the West that was introduced in the Wild West shows and exhibitions—the cowgirls and ranch women. These women were often on equal footing with their male counterparts even though a significant percentage of the men never particularly welcomed them into the sport. What the ladies brought to the Wild West Shows and then to the rodeos, along with their competitive spirits, was courage and grit that eventually, though begrudgingly, won over most of the cowboys. Although it was men who eventually came to dominate rodeo—even today most people think of cowboys, not cowgirls, when they think about the sport—in the early days it was the cowgirls who brought the "color, dash, and flare" to the arena and very often drew the crowds. Many shared the arena with the men, making few distinctions as they rode bucking horses, roped and bulldogged steers, and "raised hell for leather" in a series of daredevil events like the relay races, often actually competing against the cowboys.

Women showed off their skills in shooting, trick riding, relay races, roping, steer wrestling, and riding the rough stock and a whole new list of names began to emerge: gals like Annie Schaffer, Lulu Parr, Bertha Blancett, Mildred Douglas, Mrs. Ed "Maggie" Wright, Kitty Canutt, Prairie Rose Henderson, Dorothy Morrell, Tad Lucas, Lucille Mulhall, Bonnie McCarroll, Fox Hastings, Florence Hughes Randolph, Vera McGinnis, Bonnie Gray, Opal Woods, Marie Gibson, Fanny Sperry Steele, Lorena Trickey, Ruth Roach, Marge and Alice Greenough, Mabel Strickland, and countless others. These women began to receive notoriety that previously had been reserved only for the men.

From about 1900 to the beginning of the 1930s, the rodeo cowgirls competed in the same rodeos as the men, vying for cash prizes and equal fame. It's been speculated that those cowgirls were probably our first professional women athletes. Coupled with the likes of Annie Oakley, who toured with Buffalo Bill for sixteen years, and other female stars of the Wild West shows, new opportunities were created for those women athletes with widespread popular support from the public.

Many of the earliest rodeo cowgirls actually got their start on family ranches, the Wild West shows, and even circuses. They were the true heirs to the pioneer women who settled this country, showing the same grit and determination as the women who trekked west half a century earlier. When the Wild West shows began to fade, many of the cowboys and cowgirls drifted to the rodeo arena, the natural next stop for them—a place where they could utilize the skills that they had honed in the touring shows and learned on the home ranch.

Soon after World War I ended, it was actually the new motion pictures that had an enormous impact in the closing of most Wild West shows. Motion pictures displaced the cowgirls and cowboys, because the public could now see them and the action more frequently and with wonderful scenery at the local movie house. It was easier to shoot a movie and far less expensive then staging and touring a grandiose Wild West show. It should come as no surprise that the first movie was a western.

Annie Shaffer of Arkansas, considered by some to be the first of the bronc-riding cowgirls, had her start in the Buffalo Bill Wild West Show but not in actual rodeo competition. She rode her first bronc at a Fort Smith, Arkansas, rodeo in 1896, but as an exhibition ride, not as a competitor. Lulu Belle Parr, another of the early stars,

BELOW: Seven cowgirls with a burro before they compete in the bucking horse contest at the Weiser Round-Up in Idaho, c. 1915. Among the cowgirls are Ruth Roach, Bonnie McCarroll, Fox Hastings, and Rose Smith.

was born in 1878 in Iowa and raised in Wyoming. She first performed with several Wild West shows and rode buffalo, wild steers, and bucking horses before she became known as a first-class bronc rider who rode with hobbled stirrups.

It was in the early 1900s that the first cowgirls entered the bronc-riding competition despite protests from the cowboys and complete confusion on the part of the judges. At Cheyenne's Frontier Days, Prairie Rose Henderson (born Ann Robbins, the daughter of a Wyoming rancher) entered the bronc-riding contest despite the protests of the judges who found that they had no rules or even a legal right to exclude her. It's been reported that she put on such an outstanding ride and created such a sensation among the spectators and the press, even though she didn't win, that other rodeos quickly added a cowgirl's bronc-riding competition as a special event. What makes this so interesting is that there was no shortage of women who wanted to enter such a rough-and-tumble contest.

Prairie Rose had a much tougher ride coming up. In the 1930s she headed into a Wyoming blizzard one night on horseback and never returned. Her body was found years later, identified only by the trophy buckle she was wearing, earned at one of her earlier rodeos.

Tillie Baldwin ✦ One of the most interesting cowgirls from the early period is Matilda Winger, who rode to fame as Tillie Baldwin. She was born in Avendale, Norway, in 1888 and immigrated to New York when she was fourteen. Though initially speaking no English, she began a career as a hairdresser. On a trip to nearby Staten Island, she came upon a group of girls from Hollywood who were there practicing trick riding and bronc riding. As she watched she became fascinated and it wasn't long before she was hooked. With the help of some friends and lots of hard work, she became an accomplished horsewoman. After getting very comfortable with her riding, she was able to teach herself enough tricks on a horse that she could get a job in one of the smaller Wild West shows. She joined up with Captain Jack Baldwin's show, and the story goes that she changed her name to Tillie Baldwin just because she liked the sound of the name. There is no evidence that she ever had a relationship with Captain Jack. By 1912, she was so skilled that she became the star of the bigger and more prestigious 101 Ranch Wild West Show. The same year she took a leave of absence from the show to enter the Pendleton Round-Up where she won both the trick riding and the cowgirl's bronc-riding contests. By 1913, she started her rodeo career professionally at the Winnipeg Stampede in Canada. In 1914, again at Pendleton, Tillie Baldwin even put on a demonstration of bulldogging, not generally considered a woman's event.

During a long career, she was a roper, a trick rider, entered relay races, rode bucking horses, and was one of a number of cowgirls who could actually wrestle a steer. The relay races were particularly thrilling for the cowgirls and they were an even bigger draw with the crowds. The women rode one horse one lap around the track, switched to a another horse for a second lap, and rode a third horse

ABOVE: Cowgirls in the 1920s wearing a variety of outfits, including the "woolie" chaps and several hat styles. Photo by O'Neill Photo Co., courtesy of the Professional Rodeo Cowboys Association.

for the final lap and sprint to the finish line. Baldwin, like so many of her contemporaries who were outstanding horsewomen, excelled at those relay races.

To many, the most exciting part of the relay race was the changing of the horses since this was a timed event and even seconds could mean the difference between winning and losing. Depending on the track and the rider, there were several ways to make the change from one horse to the next. One method was simply to stop the horse, dismount, and jump into the saddle of the next horse. A second option was to pull the first horse to a stop so that its head rested on the rump of the next horse. The rider then "pony expressed" from one horse to the other without touching the ground. A third way to make the exchange was simply vaulting from one horse onto another. All three techniques were obviously very exciting and had the fans standing, yelling, and cheering the cowgirls on.

In 1941, Tillie Baldwin retired and married William C. Slate of Essex, Connecticut. She died at age seventy in 1958. Tillie Baldwin is said to be one of the few cowgirls who rode their broncs "slick," that is, without tying or hobbling their stirrups under the horse's belly. There weren't very many women who rode that way—the way the men were eventually required to ride—but the list did include legendary performers like Fanny Sperry Steele, Bertha Blancett, and Nettie Hawn.

Bertha Blancett

Bertha Blancett ✦ One of the most talked about and admired of the early women bronc busters was Bertha Kaepernik Blancett. In 1904, Bertha Kaepernik rode a horse from Sterling, Colorado, to Cheyenne, Wyoming, and put on an exhibition riding a bucking horse, becoming the first female bronc rider at the acclaimed Cheyenne Frontier Days.

Blancett was born in Colorado ranch country in 1883. From early childhood she was an outstanding rider, taught by her rancher father. In her 1904 trip to Cheyenne, she put on a sensational bronc ride in rain and mud that was so bad many of the veteran cowboys refused to compete under those conditions in their own event. That ride solidified her reputation although she continued to build on it. In 1906, she joined Pawnee Bill's Historic Wild West Show and then left to hook up with the Miller Brothers 101 Ranch Show where, in 1909, she met and married her husband, world champion bulldogger Del Blancett. Amazingly, she began

ABOVE: Bertha Blancett, on "Snake," competing in the bucking horse contest for Champion of the World at Pendleton in 1913. She is riding in a split skirt. Blancett was inducted into the National Cowgirl Hall of Fame in 1999.

hazing for him in the bulldogging, not a job usually considered suited for a woman.

In 1912, they, along with other rodeo performers, traveled to Australia with the Atkinson Show. After they returned to the states, she and Del entered and won at rodeos all over the country. At Pendleton alone, she won bucking horse championships in 1912 and 1914, and it was in 1914 that she was just twelve points away from winning the All-Around Championship. That spooked

The excitement of the crowd was almost indescribable, and it went on from one rodeo to the next. Just about every one of those brave, tough, and exciting women drew that kind of reaction from the stands.

the cowboys so badly that they got the rodeo committee to change the existing rules, and had the lady's events separated from the men's.

Soon the Blancetts moved to Hollywood where they became friends with western stars like Hoot Gibson and Tom Mix. Bertha, using her considerable horsemanship skills, became a stunt rider in the movies. During her career she was outstanding as a bronc rider, trick rider, roper, and in a number of horse racing events, particularly the relays. Del's career ended abruptly after he joined a Canadian cavalry outfit. He was killed in 1918 by a German sniper while serving with the elite Lord Strathmore Horse Unit in France during World War I. Bertha never remarried.

The war had a big effect all over the country, but the rodeos went on because there was always the feeling that everyone needed some sort of entertainment during the hard times. At Pendleton, Yakima Canutt even competed in his sailor's uniform because he was actually on leave from the navy base at Bremerton, Washington. The Oregon Troop D, which was part of Battery D, 148th Field Artillery, had a picture of a cowboy on a bucking horse and the words "Let 'er Buck" painted on the battery's guns, tractors, and wagons. In a real show of support for the war effort and our troops, the Pendleton Round-Up committee took all of the profits from the 1918 rodeo, $5,098.77, and donated them to the Umatilla County Chapter of the Red Cross.

After Del's death, Bertha lost her competitive fire and left the competition of the rodeo circuit. But she loved the sport, and a few years later she returned as a pick-up rider—someone who picks the rough string riders off their horses at the buzzer. It was remarkable that the cowboys had enough confidence in a woman to trust her to do this difficult and dangerous job, a job requiring horsemanship and considerable strength. In 1934, at the age of fifty, Bertha Blancett retired to her home in Porterville, California, and died there at the age of ninety-six, leaving a legacy as one of the pioneers of women's rodeo competition. Before her death, she received an extraordinary honor in 1961, when she was selected as the Grand Marshal of the Westward Ho! Parade, one of the only women ever selected for this honor at Pendleton.

ABOVE: Mildred Douglas, "Champion Lady Bronc Rider" in a fringed leather outfit, 1918. In 1988, she was voted into the National Cowgirl Hall of Fame.

Mildred Douglas ◆ Another of the early cowgirls with a life equally as fascinating in and out of the arena is Mildred Douglas. This champion bronc rider left her East Coast finishing school after learning to ride and jump at Minnie Thompson's indoor arena in Bridgeport, Connecticut. She joined the Barnum and Bailey Circus and then hooked up with the 101 Ranch Wild West show as a rough stock rider.

It was there that she met her first husband, bronc rider Tommy Douglas. In 1916, she rode her first bronc at the Royal American Livestock Show in Kansas City and by 1918 she had won championships in Cheyenne and Pendleton. During her career she was always easily identified by her flashy dress (as were many of the cowgirls) including her fringed split skirts and fringed vests.

When you think back to the early days when women were performing in the arena, you can almost imagine the noise the crowd made—the cheering, the yelling—and the show of appreciation after the ladies had completed their events, particularly the exciting and dangerous relay races and the bucking horse competitions. The excitement of the crowd was almost indescribable and it went on from one rodeo to the next. Just about every one of those brave, tough, and exciting women drew that kind of reaction from the stands.

Although Douglas was declared the World Champion Girl bronc rider, like many of the other rough stock riders—men and women—she headed for Hollywood in 1917. Once she settled in she worked in the growing film industry and appeared in a few films, including *The Stage Coach Race*. She made several movies with Tom Mix, and it was through that association that she met and married her second husband, Pat Chrisman, the trainer of "Tony," Tom Mix's Wonder Horse. But Hollywood didn't seem to live up to her expectations, so she returned to the Wild West show circuit where she once again became a big star. At the age of fifty-nine Mildred Douglas left the rodeos and Wild West shows to fulfill another of her girlhood dreams and become a nurse. She did that successfully for the next twenty years.

Lucille Mulhall ✦ Lucille Mulhall was born in 1885 on an 80,000-acre family ranch near Guthrie, Oklahoma. She was the daughter of Zack "Colonel" Mulhall, a man with absolutely no military background, who started a series of roping and riding contests in 1899, calling his organization "The Congress of Rough Riders and Ropers." By the time Lucille was seventeen she could rope as well as most men and twice broke the world record in steer roping. Her skill with a rope was so great that she could rope as many as eight horses at one time as they were ridden past her at a gallop. This cowgirl once roped a wolf or a coyote (it depends on who is telling the story) as part of a bet with Teddy Roosevelt. Roosevelt lost a new white Stetson.

In 1905, Colonel Mulhall produced one of the first cowboy extravaganzas in New York City's Madison Square Garden. It was at that exhibition that his daughter Lucille made such a hit as a trick rider and roper that before she left New York she was acclaimed as "The Greatest Horsewoman in America." Later in Fort Worth, she roped and tied three steers in a total of three minutes and thirty-six seconds, winning the $1,000 purse and the title "Queen of the Range." It's been said that during her illustrious career, Lucille Mulhall created more interest in the cowgirl than any other woman, either on the circuit or off, beating the best cowboys as she regularly competed in rodeo arenas around the country. As a consequence of some of her exploits, the beloved title of "cowgirl" was born. In 1899, fellow roper and Oklahoman Will Rogers saw her perform in St. Louis at the age of fourteen in one of her father's shows; he called her a "cowgirl," and that was the first time the title was ever used. Mulhall took part in roping contests at Cheyenne, Calgary, Fort Worth, and Pendleton and was certainly an inspiration to other women who wanted to or already did take part in the competitive rodeo world.

In 1919, Lucille married Tom Burnett, son of the legendary Texas rancher and oilman Burk Burnett, who owned the fabled 6666 Ranch near Guthrie, Texas. The marriage only lasted a year, and around 1920 she retired from the rodeo arena and returned to her native Oklahoma. The week of Christmas 1940, at the age of fifty-six, the car Lucille was riding in with three friends was hit by a truck. She died in the crash, about a mile from home.

Eloise Fox Hastings ✦ Of the early cowgirls, Eloise Fox was another colorful woman. Born in Texas and raised in California, Eloise ran away from home to join the Irwin Brothers Wild West Show when she was fourteen years old. While she was with the show, she competed in bronc riding and trick riding, performing all over the United States as well as in Mexico, Canada, and London. She married bulldogger Mike Hastings, a cowboy so well respected on the circuit that they called him the "Tarzan of the doggers," and "the Iron Man of steer wrestling." Eloise Fox dropped her first name and took his last name and was known thereafter as Fox Hastings.

One of her earliest attempts at bulldogging occurred at the Houston Rodeo and Stock Show in 1924. Periodically Hastings was referred to as the world's only lady bulldogger, although there were a few others in the various shows traveling around the United States and competing in rodeos. Sometimes she even competed wearing a football helmet, not something that was often seen in any of the events in the early days of rodeo. Protective gear was years away. Women typically wore split skirts with no protective vests or any other noticeable outside protection. When you consider that today, in rodeo, the average bulldogger is built like a National Football League tight end, usually way over six feet tall and topping 200 pounds, it is even more remarkable that Fox Hastings, not anywhere near that size, could compete and even have the success that she did. There is no doubt that she was strong and had the will. In addition to gaining instruction and encouragement from her husband, when it came down to essentials, she certainly had to have the desire to be successful.

In 1934, in an interview with *Hoof and Horns*, a magazine that at the time was unofficially recognized as the voice of rodeo, she gave an explanation for her participation in bulldogging. "I like bulldogging better than bronc riding. Bronc riding is a question of strength and endurance, but in bulldogging you don't tackle two steers exactly alike, you have to learn the difference in the animal's size, strength, formation of the horns, build of neck and shoulders and a lot of things. And every move has to be perfectly timed to a split second." Once at Pendleton she competed for several days with almost unbearable pain caused by three broken ribs.

Unfortunately her life ended in great tragedy that had nothing to do with rodeo. In the 1940s Fox Hastings developed tuberculosis, which did eventually go into remission. But soon after that, her husband Mike died. A couple of weeks later, in a hotel room in Phoenix, Hast-

LEFT: Fox Hastings, Mabel Strickland, and Bea Kirnan together at a San Antonio, Texas, rodeo, c. 1925.

ings committed suicide, leaving a note that read, "I didn't want to live without my husband."

Accidents in the Arena ✦ Women and rodeo were not always a smooth marriage. Rodeo certainly wasn't without its hazards, although the public couldn't get enough of the arena action. There were many tragedies, some causing serious injuries and others causing death. In fact there are records of at least seven cowgirls having fatal accidents while competing in bronc riding. It was in 1929 at Pendleton, Oregon, that Bonnie McCarroll, weighing barely 100 pounds, thirty-two years old, and a very popular and successful bronc rider, was killed. Bonnie had drawn a particularly tough mount and soon after the ride began, she lost control of her rein, got her feet tangled in the hobbled stirrups, and was thrashed about violently until she finally was flung to the ground and dragged around the arena. She was taken to the hospital where she died eight days later. The great irony of that tragic event is that McCarroll and her husband Frank—who was a pretty good bulldogger, once owning the world record time of eight seconds flat—had decided to retire after Pendleton, taking their winnings to decorate a new home they had just purchased.

Women and rodeo were not always a smooth marriage. Rodeo certainly wasn't without its hazards, although the public couldn't get enough of the arena action.

Cowgirls meeting in the 1920s. Note the number of the ladies wearing bloomers, a very accepted dress for the cowgirls at that time. From left to right: Rene Hafley, Fox Hastings, Rose Smith, Ruth Roach, Mabel Strickland, Prairie Rose Henderson, Dorothy Morrell. Photo by Doubleday, courtesy of the Professional Rodeo Cowboys Association.

Although Bonnie McCarroll was the last of the lady bronc riders to be killed in the arena, twelve years earlier, in 1917, Mrs. Ed (Maggie) Wright was killed in Denver very soon after she had won the Ladies Saddle Bronc contest at Cheyenne. Some reports suggest that she was actually riding a bronc for a Hollywood movie company when the horse fell backward over a fence, fracturing her skull.

There were, of course, other accidents involving women, not all fatal. Harold Hartle, an old cowboy and lifelong resident of Pendleton, recalls in an interview for the Jory oral history book, a story about an injury in 1912, to the redheaded rider Ella Lazinka. "When she got hurt in one of the first relay races held here at the Round-Up, the arena had a wooden fence, and she was entered in a relay race. Her horse crowded that fence, and a 2x4 was on top; a sliver in that 2x4 caught her leg and ripped her leg pretty bad. She was laid up for quite awhile. Her mother stopped her racing after that. She was never allowed to race again." Together with her horse, "Froggy," Ella not only finished the race but won. It took thirteen stitches to close her wound and she was an invalid for the next six months.

After Bonnie McCarroll's death, Pendleton stopped having cowgirl bucking events, following the lead taken by Cheyenne the year before. It wasn't too long after Pendleton that rodeos across the United States and Canada adopted that same policy and that was the beginning of the end for the cowgirl's full participation in a variety of rodeo events. Although women's rodeo would have a

RIGHT: One of the best of the early cowgirls, Tad Lucas, on a saddle bronc named "Juarez" at a rodeo in Salt Lake City, 1925. She was inducted into the ProRodeo Hall of Fame in 1979 as a Notable and the National Cowgirl Hall of Fame in 1978.

revival many years later, it has never achieved the success or popularity that it had up to the tragic death of Bonnie McCarroll in 1929. Except for barrel racing, most rodeo fans never get to see women compete unless it is in an intercollegiate or high school rodeo, on the senior pro rodeo tour, or some of the ranch rodeos or rodeos for kids throughout the country. And these gals almost never compete in the rough stock events. They rope, do pole bending, barrel race, and goat tie but never ride broncs, bulls, or steer wrestle, except on the relatively very small circuit of the Women's Professional Rodeo Association (WPRA) All Women's Rodeo. There are about twenty of those rodeos held each year across the United States.

Women's Professional Rodeo Association ✦ The
Women's Professional Rodeo Association (WPRA) was started in 1948 by a group of Texas ranch women who wanted to add "a little color and femininity to the rough-and-tumble sport of rodeo." Today they have more than 2,000 members.

In 1947, twenty-five-year-old Nancy Binford, who went on to ride bulls, and nineteen-year-old Thena Mae Farr organized what turned out to be the first competitive all-girl rodeo as part of the Amarillo, Texas, Tri-State Fair. After much skepticism by the city fathers, the girls were able to get the go-ahead to hold their rodeo, and with minimal financial backing they drew seventy-five entrants from Texas, New Mexico, Missouri, and Oklahoma to compete in bareback riding, calf roping, barrel racing, cutting, and team tying. Entry fees were a modest $5 to $15 per event and the total payout was an equally modest $1,260, with the All-Around Champion also taking home a horse trailer. The rodeo was very successful, playing to standing-room-only crowds. The success in Amarillo led to the 1948 formation of the Girls Rodeo Association. Their goal was "to give women legitimate, honest opportunities to compete in all-girl rodeos as well as establish an alliance with the RCA (Rodeo Cowboys Association) to host women's events

their Women's National Finals Rodeo in Fort Worth at the Cowtown Coliseum, and their 2005 finals was televised on the RFD cable channel.

Then out of the blue, the rodeo world was completely taken aback by the story of twenty-three-year-old Kaila Mussell of Chilliwack, British Columbia. In 2002, Kaila made some gender history when she entered the Championship Indoor Rodeo at Prineville, Oregon, on a PRCA permit. This was her first rodeo, and she wound up tying for fourth in the saddle bronc event with a score of sixty-nine points on a bronc named "Siesta Sundowner." Twenty-six contestants were entered, Kaila being the only female. "I just got my permit this year so that was my first PRCA rodeo. First time I entered I placed, so that was pretty neat." Her goal, she says, "is to be the first female to make the Wrangler NFR (National Finals Rodeo)." Times change but somehow they seem to stay the same. On March 9, 2003, at the Okeechobee Cattleman's Spring Rodeo in Florida, Kaila filled her permit.

To fill a permit, a contestant must earn $1,000 in his or her respective event. Once this amount is achieved, a contestant is then considered a full member of the PRCA. Kaila Mussell is now a full member.

in conjunction with RCA-sanctioned rodeos." Rodeo for women was back on track and today has an active, if still small, rodeo circuit.

The standard events at a WPRA All Women's Rodeo are bareback riding (the ladies use a two-hand rig), tiedown calf roping, breakaway calf roping, bull riding, and team roping. They describe their tour as "the classic rodeo events feminine style," by women who "do it for the love of the sport." There isn't enough prize money to enable any of the cowgirls to pursue their careers full time—they all have to have day jobs—but don't be misled. These women are tough and very athletic. They hold

Mabel Strickland ❖ Back to the ladies in the famous married cowboy-cowgirl couples from the earlier period, one of the great woman steer wrestlers of rodeo was Mabel DeLong Strickland. Once referred to as the "Crown Princess of Rodeo," it's been estimated that Mabel Strickland was the most photographed of all the cowgirls. She was described as a gal who "looks more like a Follies beauty then a champ cowgirl." Mabel Strickland was actually on the cover of the 1924 and 1926 Cheyenne Frontier Days souvenir programs, which is the only time that a cowgirl has ever been featured on the cover. In 1927, she was chosen as the Queen of the Pendleton Round-Up.

She was born Mabel DeLong in 1897, at Wallula, near the Columbia River in Washington state. Her rodeo career began at the age of thirteen when she decided to ride in the relay races in Walla Walla, Washington, near her home. She won the championship at that event in 1913, 1914, and 1915. As her career took off, she also won the Denver Post Ladies Relay Race at Cheyenne in 1922 and 1923, and in 1925 she won the Ladies Saddle Bronc Riding championship. She won five relay championships along with five second-place finishes at Pendleton from 1916 to 1923. While she was winning at Cheyenne, she also managed to find herself a husband, a fine All-Around Champion cowboy named Hugh Strickland.

Hugh was born in Owyhee County, Idaho, in 1888 and worked with wild horses on his father's ranch from the time he was just a youngster. He won the bronc-riding contest at Cheyenne in 1916 and 1920, and he won at Pendleton in 1918 and 1921. During his career, Hugh rode saddle broncs, roped steers and calves, bulldogged, and did some trick roping and riding. As he got older he became a very successful team roper. Hugh had a distinguished career until he broke his leg at Monte Vista, Colorado, in 1927. It didn't heal properly, and despite the fact that he was wearing a brace, he had a second break to the same leg at Ventura, California, that spelled the finish to his bronc-riding days. He did, however, continue on the circuit as a roper. Reba Perry Blakely, herself a member of the Cowgirl Hall of Fame in Fort Worth, Texas, said this about Hugh Strickland: "Hugh Strickland saved my life at a show. I was trick riding and my horse tried to savage me. Hugh yelled at him and he straightened up. Hugh laughed easy and he was a joking man. He could have you laughing. He was #1—the best rodeo manager God ever invented."

> **Mabel was so good that one frustrated cowboy asked Hugh to see what he could do about getting Mabel to quit competing against the men.**

Mabel, tutored by Hugh, became the leading cowgirl steer roper, regularly beating the cowboys she competed against, often in record-breaking times. Yet she was just 5'4" and never weighed over 112 pounds. In Dewey, Oklahoma, she roped and tied a steer in 21.1 seconds, a time that set the standard for years. Earlier, at Pendleton, she had actually roped and tied a steer in 18 seconds. Mabel was so good that one frustrated cowboy asked Hugh to see what he could do about getting Mabel to quit competing against the men. She didn't. Mabel also rode broncs and bucking steers, a precursor to bull riding. In fact, she actually did ride a bull at the Tucumcari New Mexico Roundup. And like so many of her contemporaries on the rodeo circuit, Mabel did a brief stint in Hollywood, as a stunt rider and even had a bit part in a Bing Crosby movie, *Rhythm on the Range*.

When both Hugh and Mabel's arena careers were mostly over, Hugh, in 1941, died abruptly of a heart attack in Burbank, California, before he reached his fifty-third birthday. Mabel remarried and settled in Buckeye, Arizona, where she lived a quiet life until her death in 1976 at the age of seventy-nine.

Fanny Sperry Steele

Fanny Sperry Steele was a Montanan through and through. She was born, raised, and died in the Treasure State. As the fourth of five children born on a small horse ranch in the Bear Tooth Mountains north of Helena in 1887, she started breaking her own horses as a little girl so that she could ride the eleven miles to the nearest school. When she was twenty-five she entered her first rodeo at Calgary and won the Women's Saddle Bronc World's Championship, the first year it was held, and took home her trophy and $1,000. Steele became known for never using hobbled stirrups or "cheat straps," which were common among most of the lady bronc riders. She won Winnipeg in 1913, the same year that she married the bronc rider and rodeo clown W. S. (Bill) Steele. Fanny and Bill continued to rodeo. She entered the bronc-riding competition and relay races at Pendleton, Kansas City, Great Falls, Miles City, and other rodeos as they traveled all over the country, competing and winning. Her reputation as one of the smoothest riders on the circuit became legendary. Willard Porter says that "out of no more than a dozen turn-of-the-century lady bronc riders, Fanny Sperry was the best and the most dedicated to her rough-and-tumble trade."

The Steeles also performed with the Miller Brothers' 101 Wild West Show and the Irwin Brothers Wild West Show. After the Bozeman Roundup in 1925, at the age of thirty-eight, Fanny retired from competition, and she and Bill became stock contractors, providing horses and bulls for rodeos all over the West. They had decided to settle down a bit and buy a ranch near Helena, primarily because Bill was already in poor health. But Bill Steele died in 1939, and Fanny went on to become one of only four women in the United States to be a licensed outfitter-guide, a career she pursued successfully for many years. Fanny Sperry Steele died in 1983, six weeks before her ninety-sixth birthday.

In 1993, Paul Zarzyski, one of the best and certainly the most creative poets on the Western music and poetry circuit—a former bareback rider himself and like Fanny Sperry Steele, a true Montanan—wrote the following poem that was later turned into a song to commemorate the legacy of this Hall of Fame rodeo cowgirl:

> *Fanny Sperry Steele*
> *As she swung her mom's bandana*
> *And toddled toward a bronc*
> *Her daddy swore she'd fork a horse*
> *'fore she was weened.*

She won the world in 1912
At Calgary's first stampede
She won again in Winnepeg
on Midnight in '13.

Sitting pretty in that photo
she's got her toes turned out
while Blackie's climbin'
phantom ladder in the air.

A fraction of a second
Caught 80 years ago
When Fannie rode them slick and clean
and pins flew from her hair.

Chorus: "Prairie Rose" Henderson, Vera Maginnis, Goldie St. Claire, Kitty Canutt

Buckin' Hoss Suffragettes
Calling their own shots
Their men cheered them on
From back of the chutes.

"I don't want to go to heaven,
If there's no horses there,"
Fannie in her nineties
Would tell it to you straight.

She ran Montana mustangs
Beneath the sleeping Giant
She'd already ridden thru
The pearliest of gates.

Chorus: Bonnie McCarroll, Dorothy Morrel, Ruth Roach, Tad Lucas, Kitty Canutt

Buckin' Hoss Suffragettes
Calling their own shots
While their men cheered them on
From the back of the chutes.

Vera McGinnis ✦ The story of Vera McGinnis, whose rodeo career lasted from 1913 to 1934, is remarkable. McGinnis, who was a jockey and one of the very best relay racers, also rode broncs and wild steers, did Roman racing, was a trick rider, and even rode bucking bulls. She has been given credit for inventing the flying change in the relay races and ranks with the best among the band who symbolizes these extraordinary early women of rodeo.

Vera was born in Missouri in 1892 and her life riding started at the age of three when her family moved to Clayton, New Mexico. Nicknamed "Mac" by her rodeo compadres, Vera won her first flat race in 1913 and from there gained a reputation as a first-class jockey. She even competed against men on the 1916 Colorado racing circuit, opening the way for women jockeys to compete against the men. In 1924, she was part of the rodeo Tex Austin brought to London and won two championships. She also introduced a new style of women's dress—long pants. After the rodeo was over she traveled throughout Europe and Asia displaying her abilities for trick riding and racing. In 1926, she became the first woman to win all four days of the Pendleton Round-Up.

In 1934, misfortune struck and ended her rodeo career. In a racing accident she sustained a collapsed lung, three broken ribs, a broken hip, a broken neck bone, and a broken back in five places when a horse named "China Rose" somersaulted on top of her. The doctors thought that she would never walk again, but Vera left the hospital six weeks later, on her feet. Although she couldn't rodeo again, she went home to her ranch and lived a quiet life, tending her horses; within six months she was riding again. Before she died in 1990, at the age of ninety-eight, she was inducted into the Cowgirl Hall of Fame and the National Cowboy & Western Heritage Museum's Rodeo Hall of Fame.

Press Coverage
✦ While the fans were exceptionally receptive to seeing the cowgirls perform in the arena, the press was not always so appreciative of their grit and determination. Julie Wells, in writing the history of women's rodeo for the WPRA, points out that, "Newspaper and magazine coverage reporting on women in early rodeo was a mixed bag. Some towns gave the rodeo

competitors, perhaps they would fare better in the kitchen." And she points out that even though there were many women competing, "dozens more were left with no place in rodeo other than the spectator stands." This might be a bit overstated, however these circumstances for women in rodeo led to the future development of the WPRA.

Rodeo in the Movies
✦ That the first movie was a western seems almost logical. Two years after Butch Cassidy, the Sundance Kid, and their Wild Bunch held up their last train in 1901, Thomas Alva Edison's New York–based film company produced a nine-minute western called *The Great Train Robbery*. Despite its brief length it had all the elements of a true western, including a story of a great crime, the pursuit, and the final showdown with the robbers. Once the movie business moved to Hollywood around 1910, the westerns had better scenery, even more action, and the first western film

Some of the cowgirls thought that a "championship" might even pave the way for a career in those new silent movies that were being produced in Hollywood.

unbiased coverage, including the women's sports, but most omitted the results from the women's events as if it didn't happen. A few sprinkled coverage with dour comments and sexist overtones. More than one writer pointed out that, although the women were competent

hero—Bronco Billy Anderson, who was an extra in *The Great Train Robbery*. He went on to star in nearly five hundred short westerns based on dime novel plots, first in one-reelers and then in two-reelers; these films actually established the western as a new genre. Art Acord,

who was pretty good in the rodeo arena, had a long and successful career in the early silent westerns. In the new Hollywood films, the stories, the locales, and even the costumes all caught on with the public as stars like William S. Hart, Buck Jones, Harry Carey, Johnny Mack Brown, Tom Mix, Hoot Gibson, and others emerged to set the stage for the full explosion of the westerns in the 1930s, 1940s, and 1950s, and then onto television.

As movies became increasingly popular, rodeo was beginning to replace the older Wild West shows as live action connected with the Old West, and it had the added attraction for Americans of being a competitive sport. Along the way they added promoters, publicity, local committees, and the inception of stock contractors, men who would make certain that each rodeo had a full complement of bucking horses, steers, and bulls. The better the stock, the better the reputation of the stock contractor. Today there are nearly ninety regis-tered stock contractors in the PRCA providing broncs, bulls, steers, and calves, and their financial investment is large—an individual contractor may own up to 600 head of bulls and bucking horses alone.

Although there still wasn't enough prize money from 1900 to 1930 for the cowboys to become rodeo contes-tants full time, a fair number of top hands did emerge as stars from that period. Many consider it as a sort of "golden age" for the cowgirls, who were competing with enormous success on the rodeo circuit. Some of the cow-girls thought that a "championship" might even pave the way for a career in those new silent movies that were be-ing produced in Hollywood. Although few ever made it in front of the cameras as stars, several did have good careers as stunt doubles and extras. But the new mo-tion pictures were one of the driving forces in sustaining America's fascination with the West.

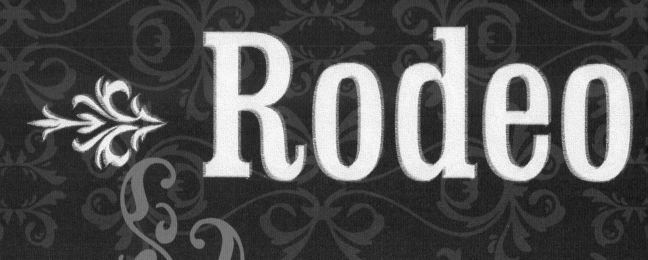

Rodeo

Six champion cowboys at a 1948 rodeo in Cheyenne: Jack Buschbom, Sonny Lavendar, Casey Tibbs, Harry Tompkins, Billy Weeks, and Red Wilmer.

Associations

As the Depression in 1929 was about to take its toll on America, rodeo had grown and was actually becoming somewhat unwieldy. There was no central organization, the cowboys were becoming unhappy about how the rodeo committees were treating them, and the rules and distribution of purses was so uneven that it would be hard to make many generalizations about what was and what wasn't. Promoters hoping for the "quick buck" started to show up and confusion seemed to be the dominant mood.

Because there was no national governing body, each rodeo functioned as a private entity and had no real connection to any other rodeo. The cowboys and cowgirls were traveling great distances, but they never knew what they would find at each stop. Maybe Cheyenne or Pendleton would be predictable and the committees would put on terrific rodeos, but what would it be like in some small town in Iowa or North Dakota or Montana? And what would it be like at a new rodeo that had no tradition and where the organizers were novices? The cowboys understood their role as entertainers, but they were often confronted with shows that were poorly organized. Not only did the facilities, purses, judges, and even the quality of the stock vary vastly from one show to another, but each rodeo could award titles like "World's Best," "World Champion," "Best Bronc Rider," and whatever other designation they could come up with, despite the fact that there was no general recognition for those titles. There was no individual or group to challenge the awarding of all those honors, and it became confusing to the public because no one really knew who was best at what. The committees were aware of the problem and so were the growing number of professional stock contractors.

Rodeo was still in its infancy in 1929, but over the previous several decades big strides had been made to ensure the public of a more complete and professional show. Even though the judges were getting better, there were still some towns that just asked local merchants, mechanics, grocers, politicians, sheriff's deputies, and other notables to do the judging—even though they were unqualified and had never ridden a bronc or roped a calf. A few had hardly even seen a rodeo. As Shirley Flynn points out about the 1915 Cheyenne rodeo, "The judges, usually prominent ranchers, were not knowledgeable in the sports involved and they waffled on decisions; ferocious arguments erupted."

In many areas the quality of the stock was improved and some of the local help in the arena and around the chutes was getting more knowledgeable, and thus were able to be of some assistance to the cowboys. The

RIGHT: L. H. 7 Ranch, Barker, Texas. Looking at the crowd and cars across the back of the rodeo chutes, c. 1930. Photo courtesy of the Professional Rodeo Cowboys Association.

problem that didn't go away was that from one location to another there was no sense of consistency with the purses, and there really was no national record keeping. It was hard to determine who actually was a champ beyond the individual show where they last competed.

In retrospect, the solution seemed easy. The rodeo committees, along with the stock contractors, got together in 1929 and formed the Rodeo Association of America (RAA). The new organization was headquartered in Salinas, California; Maxwell Mc-Nutt, a retired attorney, served as its president, and Fred S. McCargar was the secretary. What was missing was any representation from the cowboys themselves. This eventually caused both of these men to become adversaries of Everett Bowman, Hugh Bennett, and the group that was to become known as the Cowboys' Turtle Association. The Boston strike of 1936 caused a major showdown between these two organizations.

The Rodeo Association of America ✦ The goals of the RAA were simple: they wanted to correct rodeo's problems as they understood them and create more continuity throughout the country. In their own constitution and bylaws they emphasized that they organized to "ensure harmony among rodeos and to perpetuate traditions connected with the livestock industry and the cowboy sports incident thereto; to standardize the same and adopt rules looking forward towards holding of contests upon uniform basis."

Unfortunately, because the cowboys themselves had no representation in the RAA, the organization, in fact, had no legal right to speak on behalf of the cowboys or cowgirls and almost never consulted with them.

To be a member rodeo of the RAA, a rodeo had to include at least four of the following events: bronc riding, bull or steer riding, calf roping, steer undecorating, steer wrestling, team roping, and wild cow milking.

In short form, this was a fairly direct attempt to put rodeo on solid footing by providing an oversight group for the contestants and the committees, increasing the purses for the cowboys, making sure the stock was protected so as not to incur the wrath of the various humane societies the way Tex Austin had done earlier, and setting standard rules "to place such sports so nearly as may be possible on a par with amateur athletic events." Or so it seemed.

Maybe in the long run one of the most important contributions that the association made was the creation of a point system so that at the end of each year a true champion could be identified in each event and the All-Around Champion could be crowned. It was a simple system—one point was awarded for each dollar earned with no points being earned from money won at nonmember rodeos. The RAA also made it clear that no points would be awarded for increased purses over the amount listed in the original prize list. That precaution was put in place to prevent the promoters from adding to their purse at the last minute to make their rodeo more important in the selection of the champions.

The RAA made a concerted effort to standardize the rules for competitive rodeo, making sure to allow for slight variances brought about by state laws, public attitude toward rodeo, and even arena conditions. One interesting part of the RAA's rules was the expectations that they had for the cowboys, which set a pattern that is still part of the rodeo world today. It was understood from the beginning that "refusing to contest on the animal drawn by or for him; being under the influence of liquors; rowdyism; mistreatment of stock; altercation with the judges or officials; or failure to give assistance when requested to do so by an arena director, or for any reason deemed sufficient by the management, can result in withdrawal of any contestant's name and entry, barring him from any or all events, and withholding any money due him." The rules were in place and the decorum for rodeo was established, at least on paper, firmly enough that they have mostly stayed, one way or another, as an important part of the traditions of rodeo right up until the present time. It would be very hard to make a case that these codes have always been adhered to and that the cowboys have always acted the way the committees would have liked, but rodeo as a serious sport was on its way.

And yet all was not well, particularly behind the chutes. The cowboys, despite the improvements made over the entire range of the rodeo world, were unhappy about certain aspects of the organization that they felt were going against their best interests. And sometimes their own behavior went against their best interests. They remained suspicious of the committees, stock contractors, and the distribution of the money. The rules alone, no matter how hard the RAA tried, could not make the cowboys more trusting or even stop some of the rowdyism and other bad behavior. Many in the public never could get past the fact that after the Civil War, young men looking for some excitement, adventure, and maybe a turn on the outlaw trail, headed west and became cowboys. Even decades later, there were cowboys who couldn't get past that image. Their reputation as a pretty unruly bunch just would not go away. But rules only applied to the member rodeos and even though most of the rodeos did join, the RAA did not have 100 percent participation, which meant that their effectiveness could never be 100 percent. This also allowed cowboys to enter rodeos without the RAA rules. And cowboys will be cowboys!

There were, however, some very good signs. Starting in 1929, legitimate national champions were recognized and records were being kept so that there was some continuity in the rodeo world. The champions in 1929 were as follows: Earl Thode of Belvedere, South Dakota, won All-Around Cowboy and saddle bronc champion; Gene Ross of Sayre, Oklahoma, was top steer wrestler; Charles Maggini of San Jose, California, won both the team roping and steer roping titles; John Schneider of Livermore, California, won the bull riding championship; and Everett Bowman of Hillside, Arizona, was the champion calf roper.

By the next year, 1930, there were some new names and some old on the championship list: Gene Ross won the All-Around; Norman Cowan of Gresham, Oregon, was crowned champion team roper; Clay Carr

RIGHT: Cuff Burrell, a rodeo stock contractor out of Hanford, California, during the 1930s, poses with "Sonny Jim" in the late 1930s. In the 1930s he owned the bucking horse "Crying Jew," who was successfully ridden only twice out of twenty-five times in 1938. Burrell also owned bucking horses "Pancho Villa," "I Thought So," and "C. Y. Jones." Photo courtesy of the Professional Rodeo Cowboys Association.

of Visalia, California, won both the saddle bronc and the steer roping championships (he also won the All-Around Championships in 1930 and 1933); Jake McClure of Lovington, New Mexico, took the calf roping title; and John Schneider was once again the bull riding champion.

The records for bareback riding weren't kept until 1932. Bareback riding had not really been contested the way other events were, although it had appeared often as an exhibition event. By 1932, it had gained legitimate status, and Smoky Snyder of Bellflower, California, took the first crown. The next year, Nate Waldrum of Strathmore, Alberta, became the first Canadian to show up among the champions. Many more Canadians were to follow over the years in nearly every event, but particularly in the rough stock events.

In those early years some of the future big names of rodeo began to appear in the winner's circle. Fritz Truan, Louis Brooks, Bill Linderman, Bud Linderman, Hugh Bennett, Homer Pettigrew, Andy Jauregui, Pete Knight, Doff Aber, Leonard Ward, Clyde Burk, and others were showing up as consistent top hands during the 1930s, often as repeat winners. Other cowboys, including the Canadian Herman Linder, Everett Shaw from Oklahoma, Oral Zumwalt of Montana, Leonard Ward

and Alvin Gordon, both from Oregon, and Jerry Ambler from Alberta, all began to make their mark in that era of significant growth for rodeo. And yet the cowboys couldn't get past the basic inequalities they felt were still part of the way the rodeo committees ran their shows. It boiled down to whether or not they felt they were being treated fairly; they didn't think they were.

Clearly the cowboys and even the cowgirls had been at odds with the promoters for a long time. For example, the RAA announced that the individual rodeo committees would furnish the tack for saddle bronc riders, especially the saddles, so that every cowboy would have the same gear. But Hamley & Co. Saddlery had already created such a saddle for Pendleton back around 1920. Most other rodeos started to use the Hamley saddle, but it wasn't until the RAA made its regulation that it was required at all of their rodeos. That is where the term "association or committee saddle" was created. At Cheyenne, as Shirley Flynn explains, the first challenge to that rule took place in 1934. "The cowboys took issue with this immediately because, they said, not every man could comfortably and safely sit the same saddle."

Don't think, however, that 1934 was the first time that the cowboys began to voice their unhappiness with the rodeo committees. As early as 1910, the cowboys and cowgirls formed the Broncho Busters Union at the Jefferson County Fair in Colorado, demanding $5 a day for contestant wild-horse riders. Even the local newspaper reported that imposters were "threatening the respectability of the ancient and honorable profession of the real cowboy."

Alternate Organizations ✢

In 1916, the former Wild West show performer Fay Ward wrote a proposal in the *Wild Bunch,* considered the official magazine of rodeo at that time. He proposed an organization that would put on their own contests and support both the management and the contestants. Fay also had some ideas that were far ahead of his time. He wanted this new organization to take care of injured cowboys and cowgirls and to help out the families of contestants who had died. Unfortunately for rodeo, no action was taken on Ward's ideas, and it would be many years before they would be brought up again.

In 1932, another try was made to organize the cowboys, again at a major show in Colorado, the National Western Stock Show and Rodeo in Denver. The driving force and energy for the Denver organizational meetings came from M. D. Fanning, a timekeeper, who talked to the cowboys about raising the standards of their sport and providing a permanent fund to take care of the cowboys who had been injured while competing in the arena. He also believed that they could influence specific rodeos to increase their purses. This time they actually formed committees, adopted the name the Cowboys Association of America, and had ninety-five members. They even raised $300 by just passing the hat, a sum they hoped to increase before the rodeo was completed.

Over the next few years that organization slowly disappeared, but (and this is a big *but)* quite a few of the cowboys who headed up the committees were the same cowboys who led the walkout in Boston a few years later that led to the formation of the Cowboys' Turtle Association (CTA).

Lewis Bowman, Everett Bowman's nephew and author of two books filled with memories of the West and rodeo, *Bumfuzzled* and *Bumfuzzled Too,* claims that Tom McBride, a bronc rider, talked about his ideas for organizing at Prescott in July 1933. "He never sparked much interest in his radical notion until he brought it to the attention of Hugh [Bennett] and Everett [Bowman] in 1934 during the Prescott rodeo. The three of them mulled it over to some extent with some of the other cowboys."

The cowboy's frustration with low purses and other problems they had with the promoters didn't go away. The cowboys felt that the RAA did a good job of looking after the stock, the contractors, and the rodeo committees, but not the cowboys. The frustration level was real and apparently not getting any better. This all makes it a little surprising that nothing actually took hold with those early attempts at organization; that is, until you factor in the independence of the cowboys. It was hard for them to give up their "freedom." But because of the Depression and the economic troubles that were being felt all over the country, the idea of unionization or at least some kind of organization to protect the workers, or in this case, the cowboys, was at the forefront of many people's thinking, not just the cowboy's. Something had to happen, and it was in 1936 that the events just fell into place. The cowboys had tried to talk to the promoters and producers about

The cowboys still wanted a complete set of rules for each of the events, and they wanted to make major improvements in the selection and qualification of the judges.

their concerns but no one seemed to care. In the fall of 1936, at the Boston Garden Rodeo, events took place that would have an everlasting, positive influence on rodeo. The cowboys just decided that they wanted to be in charge of their own destiny, and they knew that that would never happen until they took action. And so they did.

Cowboys' Turtle Association ✦
The turmoil that took place in Boston didn't really start in Boston. Just before the Bean Town rodeo was to start, there was the equally prestigious Madison Square Garden Rodeo in New York. Both the Boston and the New York shows were produced by Colonel W. T. Johnson, generally considered the leading rodeo producer of his era. This led the cowboys to believe that if they could persuade Johnson to accept their proposals and make the adjustments that they felt were absolutely necessary, nearly all of the other producers would fall into line.

Johnson was not an ordinary rodeo stock contractor. One very glowing article, almost a PR piece, called him "the only stock magnate in the world, ruler of a cattle empire in Texas and foster-father to cowboys and cowgirls from Canada to Mexico, who produces the World's Championship Rodeo at the Boston Garden, and is truly the 'angel of the rodeo.' " The article goes on to say that "the colonel loses between $6,000 and $7,000 a year by lending money and buying railroad tickets for stranded cowboys."

Hugh Bennett, one of the top cowboys, and others tried to talk to this very same Colonel Johnson in New York but he just didn't pay any attention to them. Instead, he packed up the show that had just ended and headed north to Boston in his own train that he used to haul livestock. In an article for the *Quarter Horse News*, Walter Dennis (a close friend of Hugh Bennett's), quotes Bennett as saying: "In New York, I won the calf roping and most of the bull dogging and didn't have anything to show for it. I told Colonel Johnson just how we felt about it. I told him, 'if I had a truck and a trailer, I would go back home tonight.'. . . I told the rest of the cowboys what had happened and we decided to sign a petition to strike, if the entry fees weren't added. We made-up a petition to strike . . . and when we showed it to Colonel Johnson, he said that if we didn't enter, he would just run all of his stock into the ocean. I told him we would be glad to help."

The Colonel had forced the hands of the cowboys and they decided that it was time to act. Bennett and the others told Johnson that they were not going to show up in Boston but Johnson never did take them seriously and thought that they were bluffing. He was positive that they would be ready to ride on opening night because many of them had to compete to pick up a paycheck. He was very wrong, not just about the money but about their commitment to taking control of their own careers and the sport that they were participating in and respected. He had seriously underestimated the frustration level and the resolve of the cowboys.

There is no question that money was the major contractual issue in Boston but it certainly wasn't the only one. The cowboys still wanted a complete set of rules for each of the events, and they wanted to make major improvements in the selection and qualification of the judges. But everyone knew that money would be the deciding factor. The cowboys needed to see the prize money raised so that they could at least pay their own way. This was the era before there was any sort of sponsorships, corporate, or otherwise, so each cowboy had to cover his own expenses. The cowboys were proud of this—it allowed them to continue the tradition of independence that was so ingrained in their world.

Three days before the rodeo was to start, on October 30, 1936, the cowboys handed a petition to Colonel Johnson, signed by sixty-one participants that read: "For the Boston Show, we the undersigned demand that the Purses be doubled and the Entrance Fees added in each and every event. Any Contestant failing to sign this Petition will not be permitted to contest, by order of the undersigned."

The first name on the signature list was Everett Shaw, followed by Carl Shepard and Dick Truitt, and the remaining fifty-eight included top rodeo hands Hugh Bennett, Everett Bowman, Jake McClure, Rusty McGinty, Richard Merchant, Tom McBride, and the Canadian bronc rider Herman Linder. It is a remarkable document, in part because of its simplicity and in part because it was so radical, especially for the cowboys.

BELOW: Pictured here is a copy of the original Boston Petition signed October 30, 1936, by 61 cowboys who demanded that the purses be doubled and their entry fees be added in each and every event.

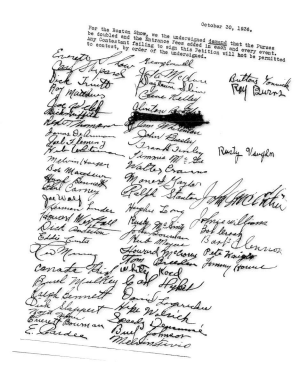

Hugh Bennett ✦ Hugh Bennett, Everett Bowman's brother-in-law, was born in September 1905 at Knox City, Texas, and started roping as a very young boy. He entered his first rodeo in 1925 at Lubbock, Texas. Bennett was big—6'4" and 225 pounds, a perfect size for a bulldogger, an event in which he also became quite proficient. In 1927, he married Josie McEnen, and they bought the Black Rock Ranch near Fort Thomas, Arizona, where they became well-known Hereford cattle raisers and breeders of fine horses. The type of horses they were raising became the American Quarter Horse, and when the American Quarter Horse Association (AQHA) was formed in 1940, Bennett was one of the moving forces. In 1964, he was elected its president. In 1986, Hugh Bennett was honored by the PRCA by being named "Man of the Year." Thirty years after his wife died, Hugh Bennett passed away in 1994. In 1979, both Hugh and Josie Bennett were inducted into the ProRodeo Hall of Fame along with Everett Bowman.

On the original document that was handed to Colonel Johnson there is a big, black cross-out. Gail Woerner, in *The Rodeo Clown*, explains that the signature belonged to Jimmy Nesbitt, who said that he had second thoughts after he signed the document because he felt that Colonel Johnson would fire him from clowning. Nesbitt stressed that he was definitely with the cowboys and that the cowboys knew that he was. He admitted later that Boston was the worst job of clowning he had ever done because he didn't want to help the "civilians" Johnson had hired to replace his cowboy friends.

OPPOSITE: Everett Bowman on a Perry Henderson bareback horse at Prescott, Arizona, in the 1920s. Photo courtesy of the Professional Rodeo Cowboys Association.

When the rodeo opened its Boston run—it was supposed to be eleven days, with fourteen performances—the cowboys refused to participate. In retaliation, Colonel Johnson attempted to get other cowboys from a Chicago rodeo and other rodeos all over the country to come to Boston. He had even offered the Chicago cowboys $500 each to travel to Boston to break the strike. At first there was a good response, but when the newly recruited cowboys heard what was actually going on in Boston they refused Johnson's request to go against their colleagues and friends. In fact, Johnson got a petition signed by 104 cowboys that said: "We, the undersigned Cowboys showing at the Chicago Stadium do hereby agree not to go to the Boston Show, unless the demands of the Cowboys now at Boston are met. The boys at Boston now, must be allowed to work and not barred from the show." Among those signing were Earl Blevins of Wyoming, the future inventor of the Blevins stirrup buckles; Homer Pettigrew, the great steer wrestler; King Merritt, a highly respected horse breeder and rancher from Wyoming; and Oral Zumwalt, a contestant and future stock contractor from Montana.

In Boston, to show their resolve, the cowboys had actually bought train tickets so that they could get home and they even had the authorizations all in order for the shipping of their horses. Lewis Bowman, Everett's nephew, tells the story in *Bumfuzzled Too* of how Hugh Bennett, one of the cowboy leaders, packed everything he owned on his roping horse, "Glassy," and led the horse down a major street in Boston, "seemingly headed out of

rodeo circuit sat in the stands on opening night and loudly booed their replacements.

According to Gene Pruett, a fine rodeo historian and former saddle bronc rider, in a 1973 article for *Persimmon Hill* titled "Cowboy Turtle Association to Big Time Corporation," the Boston newspapers reported: "At times the cowboys made such a wild demonstration that the rodeo nearly was stopped. Police repeatedly warned them, and once came close to clearing the section. . . . The saddle bronc event . . . brought down a wild din of wailing and booing. . . . 'Bring on the cowboys; show us some riders,' the cowboys in the stands cried, as rider after rider bucked off or failed to make a ride."

After the calf roping event, the manager of the Boston Garden stopped the show, gave refunds to all fans in attendance, and told Colonel Johnson to get things squared away with the cowboys or get out of town himself. The next day the cowboys announced that they were leaving Boston, although they surely had the smarts to wait around long enough to see what sort of feedback they would get from their announcement. The results were swift in coming.

By the time the next day's evening performance was to begin, Colonel Johnson had agreed to increase the purse from $7,000 to $14,000, with part of the increase coming from entry fees, part coming from Johnson, and part from the Boston Garden manager, George V. Brown,

town." Bowman points out that the diamond hitch that was used on Glassy's pack is evidence "that these rodeo contestants were bonafide cowboys of their era. It's doubtful that there were many people then who knew how to 'throw' a diamond hitch."

The refusal to rodeo by the cowboys was not about showboating—in Boston it was about money and the way the promoters were treating the cowboys. When the rodeo actually started, the only contestants Colonel Johnson could round up were a handful of stable grooms, chute hands, ex-jockeys, roustabouts, and a few Wild West show performers, all trying to ride broncs and rope calves and steers—things most of them had never done before. Sixty-one of the best cowboys on the who added $1,250 because he felt it was so important to help the cowboys meet their demands.

Colonel Johnson said, "I don't hold any hard feelings against the men; they have to earn their living by winning prize money. But sometimes they don't appreciate the difficulties of managing a rodeo."

The entire affair came down to the simple division and share of the prize money and the inclusion of the entry fees into the total purse. It was clear that the cowboys had won this confrontation. Seizing the opportunity, they decided that it was a good time to make their organization that had been so successful permanent. On November 6, 1936, the United Cowboys' Turtle Association was formed. Very soon after that first meeting they dropped the word "United" and the Cowboys' Turtle Association (CTA) was well on its way toward leaving its mark, forever, on rodeo.

An interesting side effect of all of this was that a year after the Boston troubles, Colonel Johnson sold out and the world's largest rodeo outfit went for $150,000. As part of the sale there were 150 bucking horses, 150 saddle and parade horses, Brahma steers, calves, cows, plus saddles and other miscellaneous equipment. The buyers, Mark T. and W. J. Clemens Jr. of Florence, Arizona, eventually took on a couple of partners, Everett Colborn of Idaho, and Harry Knight of Colorado. They took the name World's Champion Rodeo Company and eventually Gene Autry joined the company and became—in addition to his movie and singing career—a part-time rodeo stock contractor.

Everett Bowman ✦ Everett Bowman was born in Hope, New Mexico, in July 1899 and grew to be a rugged 6'2", 200 pounds. As a youngster he was a cowboy and he remained a cowboy for the rest of his life. By 1935, he had six World Championships—three in bulldogging, two in calf roping, and one All-Around. Early in his career he worked all the events, something you rarely see cowboys do today. After leaving the leadership of the RCA, Everett ranched with his wife, Lois, at Hillside, Arizona, just southwest of Prescott. He died piloting his own plane in a crash not far from the ranch in 1971 at the age of seventy-two. The *Phoenix Gazette* wrote: "Everett Bowman was both the George Washington and the Babe Ruth of rodeo."

LEFT: Everett Bowman, considered by many as the "Babe Ruth of Rodeo." Photo courtesy of Lewis Bowman and "Bumfuzzled."

In the CTA Articles of Association, they list ten reasons for forming the organization. A sampling of the ten gives a good idea of their goals.

1. To raise the standard of rodeos as a whole, and to give them an undisputed place in the foremost rank of American sport.
2. To advocate and work for the bettering of conditions and rules under which the members of this association are governed in the rodeo events in which they participate.
3. To adopt rules and regulations for the benefit of the members as will tend to elevate not only the class of the participants but the sport itself.
4. To protect the members of this association in seeing to it that they are paid or compensated according to the contract or arrangement which any of the members may have with any rodeo.
5. To do away with all strikes by cowboys and participants in rodeos and . . . through this organization by peaceful persuasion reach amicable understandings with rodeos to the end that the members . . . have a larger participation in the moneys paid in by the public.
6. To obtain, if possible, group accident insurance for the protection of members.

There can be no misunderstanding, no matter how you read their statements of purpose, that the CTA was by and for the cowboys first and foremost. They saw themselves as professionals and expected to be treated as professionals. They even stated that "membership in the C.T.A. is confined to professional rodeo contestants. This is to include cowgirl bronc riders, trick riders, and trick ropers." They also tried to protect their members and their organization when they stated: "No C.T.A. member shall contest at any rodeo which permits any contestant to enter who is not a member in good standing of the C.T.A."

The CTA has become one of those legendary parts of rodeo, and there are quite a few stories about how they took their rather unusual name. The stories themselves have become part of the legend and to this day not one of them is considered the definitive answer. Gene Pruett gives one explanation for the name. His story goes that at one of their meetings, one of the cowboys stood up and said, "Now let's don't give this outfit no highfalutin' name, let's take it slow like a turtle." Another story and one that has a far greater acceptance, is that the cowboys agreed that they had been so slow in getting organized that they acted liked turtles. One more story suggests that the cowboys realized that they had taken so long before they stuck their necks out for what they believed. Lewis Bowman says the name was chosen "because the cowboys realized they had been so very slow in having anything to say about their affairs. Now they had stuck their necks out and taken hold for what they believed was right. From then on they vowed to be hard to 'knock loose.' "

Whichever is the real story has probably been lost to history, but the CTA certainly solidified its place in the rodeo world and with each generation has grown in its importance. Rodeo today owes much to the cowboys of the 1930s. The turtle became their symbol and it appeared on their pin, letterheads, and all other items that required their logo.

The Turtle button, their identification pin, became a very prized possession for the cowboys. Willard Porter wrote, "Rodeo cowboys wore the Turtle button as if it were a precious gem. They pinned it to their shirt or belt, or wore it on the crown of their hat. They knew they were among an elite gathering, and they called those they had left behind (with whom they had once rodeoed) 'amateurs.' And that word carried a stigma of disrespect. Amateurs were thought of as worthless, Turtles as princely. Even today [1986], PRCA contestants collectively include most other rodeo people in this all-embracing, though literally incorrect, amateur category."

It is generally agreed that the two main leaders of the Boston revolt were Everett Bowman and Hugh Bennett. Their credentials as rodeo cowboys were about as good as it gets—Bowman, from Hillside, Arizona, was 1935 and 1937 All-Around Champion and Bennett, then from Fort Thomas, Arizona, and later from Falcon, Colorado, was 1932 Steer Wrestling Champion and 1938 Steer Roping Champion. Bowman and Bennett were also brothers-in-law and their wives, Lois and Josie, played a very valuable role in the early years for the Turtles. Although Everett Bowman was not the first president of the association (that was Rusty McGinty, who immediately after his election turned the office over to Bowman), Bowman served as the only president from 1937 until the Cowboys' Turtles Association became the Professional Rodeo Cowboys Association (PRCA) in 1945. Hugh Bennett was elected secretary-treasurer from the start.

War Heroes ✦ Fritz Truan, of Long Beach, California, the All-Around Cowboy for 1940 and a top-ranked saddle bronc rider, bareback rider, and steer wrestler, enlisted in the marines during World War II. He apparently lost his Turtle button (his number was 49) while in combat, but still, under heavy shell fire, crawled back on the battlefield to retrieve his treasured emblem. Sergeant Fritz Truan was later killed in action at Iwo Jima on February 28, 1945. He was twenty-nine years old. In his honor, the Marine Air Force Station at Kaneohe Bay in Hawaii named their rodeo arena the Truan Arena.

There is a long list of Turtle cowboys who lost their lives defending their country in World War II and Korea. During World War II, nearly 200 Turtles served in the armed forces.

At the 1937 meeting in Fort Worth, the Canadian Herman Linder was elected First Vice President and Rusty McGinty Second Vice President. The representatives of the cowboy's competitive events were as follows:

Bareback Bronc Riding..............Hughie Long,
Fort Worth, Texas
Calf Roping...........................Everett Shaw,
Stonewall, Oklahoma
Saddle Bronc Riding.................Harry Knight,
Florence, Arizona
Bull Dogging..........................Dick Truitt,
Stonewall, Oklahoma
Steer Riding...........................Eddie Curtis,
El Reno, Oklahoma

As Lewis Bowman recalls it, the "men signed the cowboys up and kicked 'em straight, (sometimes literally!). The sisters kept the books and the money in the back seat of their car and did the office work." The ladies, Lois and Josie, actually did keep those records in suitcases in their car, and they worked without pay until 1942 when Fannye Jones Lovelady took over all the duties the sisters had been performing.

Lovelady was the CTA's first and only salaried employee. She was not new to rodeo. Born and raised in the cattle business in Texas, she was still a young woman when she arrived in Arizona. She married Shorty Love-lady, a calf roper and steer roper, and together they were active rodeo participants. When the CTA became the Rodeo Cowboys' Association (RCA), the newly revised organization brought a somewhat more professional attitude to the mechanics of their association with a good foundation provided by the bookkeeping work of Fannye Jones Lovelady.

There was profound appreciation by so many of the cowboys for the work that Everett Bowman put into the formation and the success of the Turtles. Willard Porter, in his article called "Slow But Sure," quotes Phil Meadows, a one-time Arizona rancher and a rodeo historian: "Everett was a cowboy's cowboy . . . and one of the reasons was that he did more to put other cowboys in good graces than any other man. I saw too many of those no pay-off shows that Everett—and, of course, all of us—fought against. One time in Douglas (Arizona), a rodeo promoter told us there was no money to pay off with. Expenses had eaten him up, he said. But we agreed to raffle off his favorite horse. We all were in for 50 cents apiece—and his wife won the raffle."

Interassociation Conflict ❖ Despite the efforts of Bowman, Bennett, and the other cowboys, all was not going entirely as they had hoped. The conflicts with the RAA persisted and so in 1938 a convention was held in Ogden, Utah, that brought members of the RAA and the CTA together. The CTA had declared that they wanted to "raise the standards of rodeo as a whole and to give them an undisputed place in the foremost rank of American sports." They added that they wanted a fair deal for the cowboys and that meant better purses and rules that treated the contestants fairly. The friction between the RAA and

CTA was real. The RAA felt the cowboys of the CTA were treading on the power and authority that had been built up since they organized in 1929. From the cowboy's way of thinking, the RAA was essentially the organization for the rodeo committees and stock contractors while the CTA represented the cowboys. And when the CTA posted their basic four rules, the RAA was sure that there really was a conflict. In popular terms, the conflict was between labor (cowboys and cowgirls) and management (rodeo committees and stock contractors).

The CTA rules were printed in the December 1936 issue of *Hoof and Horns* magazine:

Rule I imposed a $500 fine on any cowboy or cowgirl who participated in any rodeo where the CTA had agreed to strike.

Rule II stated that the $500 fines would be put into a trust fund to be used for lawyer fees, telephone, telegrams, etc., and that a $100 fine would be paid by any cowboy or cowgirl for "disgraceful conduct" which must be proven before the Board of Directors. They also levied a $5 annual membership fee.

Rule III stated that all members had to approve a strike before a list of signatures could be sent to the committee of a rodeo whose purse was considered insufficient. It also disallowed individuals from walking out for personal reasons.

Rule IV dealt with another of the long-standing problems—judges and judging. The CTA claimed the right to "demand capable judges, and should there be judges who do not come up to this standard, the [CTA] reserves the right to send a representative to the rodeo committee to ask for a change of judges." They did agree not to interfere with an individual member's personal problems with a judge or another CTA member.

In spite of everything that the CTA seemed to be accomplishing, there were to be some very hard times ahead. A significant number of the rodeo committees didn't like the cowboys telling them how to run their shows or what they perceived to be the arbitrary way the CTA exerted its power. The Turtles often threatened strikes when they didn't get their way, and the committees finally said that they had had enough. The Pendleton Round-Up, for example, posted a sign on the rodeo office door that read, "No Turtles Need Apply." The officials at Pendleton would not permit the Turtles to pick the judges for either the 1937 or 1938 roundups so they just turned the two rodeos into amateur competitions with mostly locals and nonmember cowboys competing. And to the consternation of the Turtles, the shows proved to be great successes, in part, said Round-Up President D. W. McNary, "because of the fine performance of cowboys from our own ranges." By 1939, Pendleton and the Turtles had settled their differences, and at the four-day show that year there were 25,000 in the crowd on Saturday as a North Dakota cowboy, Bill McMacken, a Turtle, won the All-Around crown.

By 1938, several of the more established rodeos were about to quit the RAA because of the demands made by the Turtles. The controversy kept simmering, so both sides finally agreed to have the 1938 Ogden, Utah, conference to try to resolve some of the problems and come to an agreement that both factions felt they could live with. They drew up eight rules and money was still at the top of the list. Rule I stated that: "At all shows or rodeos for the year 1938, all entrance fees must be added in each event to the prize money."

Finally, the meeting in Ogden was able to bring the two organizations closer to agreement on some of the issues that bothered both sides, and though there would be periodic problems, rodeo finally began to get a grip on the events in and out of the arena. The demeanor that eventually came to dominate rodeo—square dealing and sportsmanship—took hold. Everett Bowman and Hugh Bennett ran a tight ship, but they had the respect of the cowboys and eventually learned how to be more tactful and diplomatic when they worked with the committees. The two top men even had to contend with their own cowboys, who feared that maybe they were going to be tied to the dictatorial powers of some kind of union. The independent spirit of the cowboys instinctively rebelled

Of all the stories about the organizational problems facing the Turtles in the early days, none paints a better picture of the conflicts that Bowman and Bennett faced than the story told by Lewis Bowman. "At age thirteen, I was with Uncle Everett and a cowboy friend of his in the infield of the Cheyenne Frontier Days Rodeo in 1937. The name of the friend escapes me so for purposes of telling this story of some unique TURTLE history, I'll call him Joe.

"In the course of Uncle Everett's and Joe's argument, Joe's adrenaline got much too high, he lost his cool and took a swing at Uncle Everett. Uncle Everett blocked the swing with one hand and with the other, punched Joe in the nose knocking him cold. Blood flew everywhere, and

The attitude and behavior of the cowboys had become something of an issue by itself because they were still perceived by many as a bunch of rowdy drunks who would just as soon fight as do anything else.

against such a possibility. The cowboys were apprehensive that their freedom would be taken away if they had to abide by demands of a large group or organization. Bowman and Bennett dealt with that, and because of their own rodeo backgrounds they were able to make the case for the CTA to most of the competitors.

Joe's nose was mashed all out of shape. While Joe was unconscious, laying on his back, Uncle Everett lifted the top half of him up by the shirt at his chest and dragged him as though he were a sack of potatoes to the rodeo office which was a few yards away. Most unceremoniously, Uncle Everett dropped Joe at the door, threw a fifty dollar

ABOVE: Paul Bond, a Turtle, was a bareback rider and also a trick rider, performing here at the Florida Cow Capital.

bill on to his chest and called to someone inside saying, 'Take this S.O.B. to the doctor and get him patched up; I'm sure he'll survive.'

"A couple of hours later Joe walked into our camp in the rodeo infield in a jovial mood with his nose all taped up and extending a twenty-dollar bill in his hand. He exclaimed, 'Here's your change, Bowman, I'll join the TURTLES.'

"'In that case,' Uncle Everett said, 'Keep five of the twenty dollars and put it on your initiation fee.'

"These guys remained friends from that day forward and it disturbs me to no end that I haven't been able to recall Joe's proper name. So when it is said, the TURTLES were sometimes organized by hand, I can truly say, I witnessed some of that."

It has been told many times in history that Everett Bowman was not the best of diplomats and there was no way to change his mind when he felt he was right. This characteristic in a strong leader was said to be appreciated for getting the new fledgling organization off the ground. Will Porter, editor of the *Hoof and Horns* magazine in the 1930s and later editor of the *Wild Bunch* newsletter of the National Cowboy Hall of Fame, Oklahoma City, Oklahoma, often alluded to the fact that "Everett Bowman was probably the most forceful man in rodeo history." Will elaborated in his writings about how fortunate the sport of rodeo was to have Everett "even though this dynamic cowboy won't go down in history as being its top diplomat!" However, Everett had a sincere liking for people and a chemistry about him that attracted young and old alike. This quality of his personality proved invaluable in his efforts to organize the rodeo cowboys.

Everett Bowman took a lot of criticism during his tenure as president of the CTA. Some of it was the result of his strong will, but the one thing that no one—friend or foe—ever accused him of was not having the best interests of the cowboy as his number-one priority.

Everett Shaw, one of the original Turtle members and first calf-roping director, said, "These young fellows in Rodeo now, or starting out, will never realize how much they owe to Everett Bowman. He was pretty stubborn, and sometimes he might not have been entirely right, but if he thought he was right, he stayed with it. And he stood for helping Rodeo. By the time of the Boston affair in 1936, he had been rodeoing for 15 years, and knew that the years it would take to really establish rodeo would do little to benefit him personally." When

ABOVE: Ben Johnson was the World Champion Team Roper in 1953, long before he launched a successful movie career. He is getting ready to rope at Pawhuska, Oklahoma, in 1959. He was voted into the ProRodeo Hall of Fame in 1979.

of the cowboys and cowgirls who participated in the growing number of rodeos. The purses were increased, entry fees were added to the purses, and the judging became more consistent and proficient. The contestants began to have a more professional attitude as their sport grew faster than any of them ever imagined it would.

The attitude and behavior of the cowboys had become something of an issue by itself because they were still perceived by many as a bunch of rowdy drunks who would just as soon fight as do anything else. Phil Meadows, the rodeo historian, observed that, "Many a suitcase was lowered out of a hotel window, the owner making a getaway without paying up."

By the early 1940s those attitudes were changing and the public began to see those tough hombres in a much better light. Professionalism was taking over and many of the cowboys began to view rodeo as a way to actually make a living doing something that they really enjoyed. They began to treat the sport with a far more professional demeanor and realized that if the fans liked what they saw they would come back.

Willard Porter, somewhat tongue in cheek, writes: "So, off came the stubble of beards. Bars of soap began to appear in places where cowboys lived. Old hot water heaters began to be repaired. Hats, jackets, shirts, and trousers began to be considered as adornments in addition to being functional. Boots started to take on a brighter polish." Porter comments that he saw a cowboy at a rodeo, a Turtle he knew, wearing a hip-length plaid jacket of yellow, red, tan, and black. "He made an impression on me because he looked the way a rodeo cowboy should look, the way Everett Bowman wanted all of them to look."

Shaw, a six-time world champion steer roper made that statement in 1973, he was sixty-five and the only original Turtle still an active contestant.

After all the commotion is brushed aside, several things happened that made the Turtles a strong outfit. First and foremost, it achieved its primary goal to improve the lot

Over the years the CTA had 2,022 members, all the best cowboys of its day. Jimmy Nesbitt, part of the rebellious Boston crowd but the one who scratched his name off the petition, was #1, and Wart Baughman carried #2022. There were also about 175 Honorary Turtles, including Justin Boots, Roy Rogers, Fay Ward, and Ben the Rodeo Tailor.

As World War II came to an end it seemed the time was right for rodeo to make some changes. The sport had spread its wings; it had gained a large degree of coherence, and it was just time to continue the growth. On a more practical level, the Turtles had in fact grown to the point where they needed office space and a permanent staff to keep track of all the cowboys, rodeos, and purses, to collect the dues, and to take care of all the everyday details and paperwork that the growing organization was accumulating.

The Rodeo Cowboys Association ✦ In March 1945 there was a meeting in Fort Worth, and it was decided to change the name of the Cowboys' Turtle Association to the Rodeo Cowboys Association, although that had apparently already been discussed and decided at a February meeting in Houston. There are conflicting stories about that meeting, but it was clear that some of the cowboys just didn't like the name "Turtles." A number of the cowboys claimed that the name had nothing to do with cowboys, rodeos, or the West, and many of them wanted a name that was deemed more appropriate for rodeo and one that the fans would better understand and identify with.

At the Fort Worth meeting an office was established in rented space in the Sinclair Building, and Toots Mansfield,

a seven-time World Champion calf roper from Big Springs, Texas, was elected president. He held the position until June 1951, when he retired from full-time competition and resigned the presidency because he felt the pressure from his other business interests. During his career, Mansfield had been a dominant force among the ropers. He won the calf-roping championship at Madison Square Garden seven times, Pendleton and Cheyenne three times each, and Fort Worth four times. In 1947, at Clovis, New Mexico, he won a winner-take-all steer-roping competition and took home a purse of $14,500, an enormous sum for that time.

The Rodeo Cowboys Association (RCA) was continuing down the long and difficult road that would ultimately place rodeo at the forefront of professional sports. The board of directors was elected by a vote of the entire membership, and a few weeks later at another meeting, the RCA decided to hire a business manager. The person they selected was Earl Lindsey, a Texas businessman and former employee of Gene Autry's organization. That forced Fannye Lovelady to resign. There was no direct criticism of Lovelady or the work she had done for the Turtles. Certainly there was no attempt to get rid of her because of any lack of professionalism or commitment on her part. It was just that the new organization wanted new blood, and Lindsey's job was to be greatly expanded to include being the cowboy's spokesman in negotiations with the various rodeo committees. Lindsey was also slated to be a public relations agent for the RCA.

Most everyone applauded the changes and envisioned continued and significant growth. Even *Hoof and Horns* jumped on the bandwagon, writing in August 1946: "Rodeo now ranks the second-highest sport in the entire United States and only baseball beats it; however,

While the boys were away the one thing the association worked hard to do was to keep interest in rodeo built up right to the maximum against the days "the boys would be coming back" and the promise the association made those boys is more than fulfilled.

Cowboy Champions for 1942, World Championship Rodeo Madison Square Garden, New York. Left to right: Hank Mills (bareback), James Kenney (calf roping), Colonel Kilpatrick, Jerry Ambler (saddle bronc), Roy Rogers, Erbie Munday (wild calf milking), Jack Favors (steer wrestling), Mr. Colburn (producer), and Dick Griffin (bull riding). Photo courtesy of the professional Rodeo Cowboys Association.

in the Western states and particularly the Pacific Coast states, there is no argument but that rodeo is now the No. 1 sport. Never before have there been so many rodeos, so many well planned and financially successful shows. . . . Never have the audiences been so enthusiastic; and never have the cowboys contested with such high spirit and grim determination." This was all pretty high praise, but probably quite accurate even coming from a pro-rodeo publication.

Although the changes that were underway with the formation of the RCA were generally met with enthusiasm, not everyone within the membership was so optimistic. There were members who had been part of the original sixty-one Turtles in Boston, who had rodeo careers that dated back to the 1920s, and who took a very conservative view of what was happening. They were very uncertain about what the future would hold as their organization continued to grow. Of all of the cowboys, it was Everett Bowman, the leader of the Turtles, who became the spokesman for the more conservative elements. He had resigned his position as president because he didn't like the fact that the directors, not the full membership, had decided to hire a business manager. That one decision seems to have stuck in the craw of Bowman and he was angry that the new position commanded a salary of $7,500, plus undefined travel expenses. In a statement printed in *Hoof and Horns*, he clearly stated what had been an undercurrent, particularly among the older hands: "I always felt that any time we had to go outside of the Cowboys to get someone to run the business, the thing was sunk, according to my way of thinking. I still think our cowboys are plenty capable of running their own business." This statement also makes you wonder about how much of Bowman's thinking represents at least partial loyalty to Fannye Lovelady. Loyalty was a trait very important to Everett Bowman.

Despite the opposition that never did become very widespread among the members, the RCA was off and running. With cowboys coming home

LEFT: A cover from the June 1948 *Hoofs and Horns* with Jim Egan on Bob Barmby's bull #26 and an unidentified cowboy on the bucking horse "Reservation" at Red Bluff, California, in 1948. It's a rare event to see these two in the arena at the same time. The title of the cover is "Unusual Situation." Courtesy of the Professional Rodeo Cowboys Association.

from the war and new, younger competitors ready to step in, the future began to look very bright. *Hoof and Horns* reported in 1946 in their Cowboy Association of America column: "Noticeable in the entry list of all rodeos is the large number of returned veterans from all branches of the service, the boys who had to hang up their rigging, put away their saddle and horse, and pack away the Stetsons and high heeled boots.

"While the boys were away the one thing the association worked hard to do was to keep interest in rodeo built up right to the maximum against the days 'the boys would be coming back' and the promise the association made those boys is more than fulfilled. And the way those boys just home are rodeoin', their fears of being out of practice are all proving groundless because they're in there now roping the fastest and fitting the best rides, and the list of winners at every rodeo will find the boys just home from overseas well represented."

Rodeo was about to enter a new era. Most of the cowboys agreed that "sure rodeo was getting bigger" but things had been working out pretty well under the banner of the Turtles. What they were unsure about was what changes the RCA would bring to their sport other than new offices and some more and aggressive PR. The initial goals established by the RCA appeared to be fairly close to those of the Turtles. Their objectives were still concerned with fairness to the cowboys, better purses, better judges, protection from management, and so on. Kristine Fredrikson, in her comprehensive study of rodeo, *American Rodeo: From Buffalo Bill to Big Business*, states, "The association entered into this new phase of its existence with a firmer commitment from its members . . . which placed it, for the first time, on a solid business foundation. For that reason . . . the changes were destined to bring about what the cowboys had sought to achieve since their first attempts to form a union to protect their interests and advance their sport."

International Rodeo Association ✦ It was not smooth sailing yet, though, at least not for the newly formed RCA. In April 1946, the National Rodeo Association (formerly called the Southwest Rodeo Association) and the Rodeo Association of America (RAA) voted to merge and call themselves the International Rodeo Association (IRA). With that move there were two major organizations, the RCA and the IRA, each awarding championships and each competing for whatever dollars were available at the increasing number of rodeos throughout the country.

Although there were attempts made at bringing the two organizations together, what really happened was that two separate philosophies developed side by

The trail was finally cleared for the RCA to become the only major force in rodeo and, to some, the only real organization for professional rodeo.

side. In 1947, the IRA declared that some of its rodeos would be open rodeos—rodeos that anyone could enter. On the other hand, the RCA had a policy of only allowing professionals, that is, its own members, into its shows. They considered "open shows" nothing more than amateur rodeos. A meeting between the two competing organizations was held in Stockton, California, and some agreements were reached. This quieted things down for a time, but one of the big problems was that both organizations were still awarding titles at the end of each year. In 1947, the RCA named its first All-Around Cowboy, Todd Whatley, a twenty-seven-year-old Oklahoma cowboy who competed in bareback riding, bull riding, and steer wrestling. In 1947, he won the steer wrestling competition and finished second in the bull riding competition to claim the All-Around title. So it became very clear that there were not only going to be two champions named in each event but there would also be two All-Around champions.

The naming of champions was not the only conflict between the IRA and the RCA. Money had always been an issue for the cowboys, and during the era of the Turtles the addition of the cowboy's entry fee to the purse put up by the rodeo committee added up to the total prize. The IRA wanted to count only the purse put up by the committee and not include the entry fees. Because points were awarded on the basis of one point for each dollar won, there was quite a discrepancy in the two systems, and the cowboys of the RCA felt that this would be a return to the old way of doing business that the Turtles had so vigorously fought against.

LEFT: Casey Tibbs aboard bronc "Okanogan Red" at Pendleton 1949. One of the the smoothest saddle bronc riders of all time, he was elected the ProRodeo Hall of Fame in 1979.

RIGHT: Wag Blessing, the 1947 Bull Riding World Champion, being bucked off "Crazy One," a bareback horse in Nimes Gard, France, in 1956. The rodeo was held at the 2,000-year-old Roman amphitheater. Photo courtesy of the Professional Rodeo Cowboys Association.

Late in 1950, the RCA moved their headquarters to more centrally located Denver, Colorado. Earl Lindsey had resigned and was replaced in May 1951 by Charlie Colbert, a steer wrestler from Wilson, Oklahoma, who was given the title of secretary-treasurer.

The squabbling with the IRA didn't end, although things were going well for the RCA. In the summer of 1951 the RCA reported that it would recognize as IRA All-Around champions only cowboys who had won at a minimum of three events—including at least one timed event and one rough stock event. The next year, 1952, the IRA countered by saying that the All-Around Champion had to announce their champions at the Grand National Rodeo in San Francisco and the RCA champions had to be crowned at the National Western Livestock Show in Denver. This confused the public—they wanted to know who the world champions really were and how they became world champions. And maybe more importantly, it made the cowboys angry.

By 1955, the IRA finally announced that they were no longer going to be naming champions. At least the title "champion" was going to be dropped from the awards they gave out to their top performers at the end of the year.

The RCA thought of this as a victory because they always believed that their designated champions were the only true champions. Finally, after years of conflict and confusion, the RCA event leaders were the only ones recognized as title holders. By the end of 1955, the IRA left the competitive rodeo arena. It became more of a management organization and got involved in areas such as the Miss Rodeo America pageant and other rodeo-related activities. The IRA even changed its name to International Rodeo Management. The trail was finally cleared for the RCA to become the only major force in rodeo and, to some, the only real organization for professional rodeo. The RCA proceeded down that road, cautiously but with confidence.

Post-World

War II Progress

The Grand Entry at Ellensburg, Washington, with the Indian contingent waiting outside ready to enter the arena, 1946.

By the late 1940s a new generation of champion cowboys had begun to dominate the rodeo scene. Todd Whately, Jim Shoulders, Jerry Ambler, Bud Linderman, Bill Linderman, Homer Pettigrew, Ken Roberts, Troy Fort, Harley May, Wag Blessing, Gerald Roberts, Gene Pruett, Casey Tibbs, Harry Tompkins, Don McLaughlin, Chuck Sheppard, Vern Castro, Shoat Webster, and Gene Rambo are just a few of the new names that started to turn up regularly among the winners on the rejuvenated and growing Rodeo Cowboys Association circuit.

After the war, rodeo grew at an unbroken pace, prompted in part by a variety of forces that came into play all at once. In the postwar period, people seemed to want a way to release all the pressures and sacrifices that they had made during the war, and sports—including rodeo—was a big part of that, as it always has been in America. According to Kristine Fredrikson, others even attributed the growth as part of a desire to go back to older values, a time in America's past that was then viewed, as it is now, romantically—the Old West. This rationale is a little hard to evaluate and may be a scenario drawn mostly by people who like rodeo. A third explanation is that, unlike today, Americans were not nearly as much participants in recreation as they were watchers. There weren't as many opportunities to be part of the action as there were opportunities to be spectators.

Kids growing up right after the war did not have organizations for their own age groups like Little League Baseball, Youth Football, or Little Britches Rodeo. In those days it was mostly "sandlot," and if you wanted to play, you got together with a bunch of kids and organized your own teams. If you wanted to see the best, you went to see the pros. There wasn't any television and that meant you listened to the radio or went to the ball park, the stadium, or the rodeo arena. Rodeo wasn't the only sport to show rapid growth in the late 1940s and early 1950s, but rodeo did have its share of the increasing recreational dollar.

Towns that had not had rodeos before the war were trying to become part of the growing tradition. Purses were increasing, making it even more attractive for young cowboys and cowgirls to make rodeo more than a hobby, and the public had become more accepting of the cowboys who were doing their best to clean up their image. Rodeo had spread its wings so that Canada and Australia were also part of what was becoming one of the most exciting and fastest-growing sports around.

Paul Bond, without question the dean of today's boot makers, also rode bulls, bareback horses, and did some trick roping. "When I rodeoed, both as a contestant and a contract act, I could do both at a given rodeo." He started the boot business in Nogales, Arizona, in 1946. He was also Cowboy Turtle #395. In an interview in December 2004, before his ninetieth birthday, Bond talked about the differences between cowboys and rodeo in the 1930s and

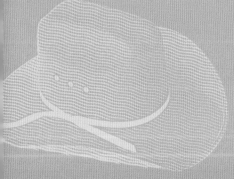

those who competed in the 1940s. After World War II, he said, calf roping got faster because the cowboys were better mounted—they began to use more quarter horses and they improved their technique, especially how they stepped off their horses. In the bronc riding contest, he said, the horses got tougher. Bond pointed out that in the 1930s there was more respect for the money because during the Depression money was so tight. This explains, in part, why the Turtles acted when they did and the way they did. In the 1930s, horses were hauled by train, by the 1940s they were hauled in early horse trailers. Rodeo, he said, did become more professional. In the 1930s rodeo was more a sport and less a business; "it was better than working on a ranch."

By the 1940s, rodeo was better organized, and Paul Bond was one of the cowboys who served on the RCA board; his term ran from 1945 to 1952. In that period, rodeo was still a growing sport but there was more money, although not enough to keep most of the cowboys from having to work at other jobs. Bond says that "lots of ranch hands rodeoed. They didn't really see themselves as pro-athletes." From his days as an active contestant, he named Dick Griffith, Earl Thode, Smokey Snyder, Wag Blessing, Bob Crosby, Louis Brooks, Homer Pettigrew, Dick Truitt, Everett Bowman, and Herman Lindner as some of the best cowboys. Bond saves some of his highest praise for Vic

Blackstone, an all-around, five-event man, who was "as good as anyone I ever saw."

In the 1950s, rodeo began to gain a new national acceptance and with that came more and more national coverage. Magazines, newspapers, and other periodicals started to have features about rodeo and many of the new emerging rodeo stars. A photograph of Casey Tibbs, the larger-than-life champion saddle bronc rider, became the face of rodeo when

RIGHT: After World War II, corporate sponsors began to discover rodeo. The 1946 World Champion saddle bronc rider, Jerry Ambler, appeared in this ad for Camel Cigarettes although he was never a smoker.

he appeared on the October 22, 1951, cover of *Life* magazine. This South Dakota cowboy was probably the most well-known cowboy of his day, and, although primarily a saddle bronc rider, he was also an accomplished bareback rider. He won the All-Around Champion award in 1951 and 1955 to go with six saddle bronc championships and his 1959 bareback crown. He began his rodeo career in 1943 at the age of fourteen and perfected one of the smoothest riding styles ever seen in the rodeo arena.

That was also a period when great bucking horses and bulls began to have almost as much notoriety as the cowboys. Even the cowgirls' barrel horses began to have an identity of their own. Anyone who is even slightly familiar with rodeo is aware of Charmayne James's super barrel horse, "Scamper," Kristie Peterson and her horse "Bozo," or Kelly Kaminski and "Rocky."

Early Bronc Riders ✦ Going all the way back to the early bronc riders at Deer Trail, Colorado, cowboys began to gain recognition for their prowess with livestock. Although most of the early names have been lost, there still are cowboys like "Booger Red" Privett, who was born in Texas in 1858. He won the first bronc ridings ever held at Fort Worth and San Angelo, Texas, and once won $1,500 for riding an outlaw bronc at San Angelo that had been brought south to Texas all the way from Montana. There seems to be little argument that Booger Red, who died in 1926, was one of the early top bronc riders. *Hoof and Horns* gives some recognition to early bronc riders such as Ben Blackburn, Doc Goodwin, Fred Bath, and others who are pretty well lost to history, although their names still appear on old rodeo records at places like Prescott, Pendleton, and Cheyenne.

Other rough stock riders and ropers who have had their places preserved in rodeo history include Harry Brannan, who was born in Wyoming in 1880 and was referred to as "the father of modern bronc riding;" Chester Byers, who probably was one of the best-known ropers in the world in the early years of the twentieth century; Lee "Babe" Caldwell, who was born in 1892, raised on the Umatilla Indian Reservation, and became one of the all-time bronc riders; and J. Ellison Carroll, who was born on a Texas ranch in 1862 and was another one of the pioneer champion ropers. In 1904, as an example of their recorded history, we know the story of how Carroll defeated Clay McGonagill in one of the biggest head-to-head steer ropings ever held. It lasted three days and Carroll averaged 40.3 seconds per head to McGonagill's 46.1.

Of course there are others. John Bowman, the 1936 All-Around Champion was a top-notch cowboy. He worked for the historic XIT Ranch in the panhandle of Texas, the Diamond A in New Mexico, and he rodeoed with Jim Brister—the 1947 champion team roper. Brister was one of the best cowboys who ever worked on Supreme Court Justice Sandra Day O'Connor's family's Lazy B Ranch outside of Duncan, Arizona. Bowman (not related to Everett) was a top calf roper and steer wrestler.

OPPOSITE: The great bucking horse "Trail's End" on May 10, 1964, the day he sold for $4,400. He had been owned by Oral Zumwalt. Photo courtesy of the Professional Rodeo Cowboys Association.

That was also a period when great bucking horses and bulls began to have almost as much notoriety as the cowboys.

Bucking Broncs ❖ In the early days of rodeo, before there were professional stock contractors, before horses were bred just to buck, and before the publicity mills could grind out the PR for the horses as well as the cowboys, broncs were a challenge, and whoever was producing a particular rodeo offered prize money to anyone who could stay on a local bronc that was considered "unrideable," or even an "outlaw." Rough horses, particularly the ones thought to be "outlaws" from this early era, were well known, and the cowboys wanted to compete on them to show off their own talents.

Names like "Tipperary," "Steamboat," "Gray Bob," "Flying Devil," "Coyote," "Prison Bars," and "Flaxie" became famous, or infamous, among bronc riders. Later on, the ProRodeo Hall of Fame (part of the PRCA complex in Colorado Springs) started to induct some of the more famous and notorious animals. Among the saddle broncs now enshrined in the Hall are "Tipperary," "Steamboat," "Midnight," "Five Minutes to Midnight," "Hell's Angel," "Descent," and "Miss Klamath." Bareback horses inducted are "Come Apart," "High Tide," "Skoal's Sip-

RIGHT: This sculpture called "The Producer" was created by Cowboy Artist of America sculptor Bob Scriver. It is of Oral Zumwalt on his favorite arena horse, "Rainbow." Zumwalt was a World Champion bulldogger before he became a top stock contractor. Courtesy of the Lowell Press.

pin' Velvet," and "Three Bars." As an example of where and how these horses became part of rodeo's legend, "Comes Apart" will serve as a good example.

This Hall of Fame inductee was foaled on the open range south of Red Lodge, Montana, along the very rugged country on the Wyoming border. He was at first put into the saddle bronc string of extremely well-respected Montana rodeo stock contractor Leo Cremer's band, but it wasn't until he went to Harry Knight's bareback string in Colorado that he began to truly stand out. He was big—he weighed about 1,400 pounds and stood sixteen hands—and so strong that an article in the *Pro Rodeo Sports News* claimed that "he pulled apart cowboy's ribs, snapped their wrists and rearranged their forearms. He jerked gloves right out of the rigging, and the stitching right out of the gloves. And when he got done turning the cowboys upside down, he turned them inside out. For the power that this horse possessed was like no other." That's a horse that created a legend.

There are other great bucking horses waiting to make the Hall of Fame. Horses of the Year like "Warpaint" (1956, 1957, and tied in 1958), 'Trails End" (tied in 1959), and "Big John" (1962 and 1963), all have a special place with the saddle bronc riders of the 1950s and 1960s.

known before he was retired in 1995 as "the world's most dangerous bull." Gavin Harvey, OLN's president, observed that their research said, "Pay attention to the

Bucking Bulls ✧ In the past several decades bucking bulls have become almost as well known as the bull riders themselves. "Old Spec," "Oscar," "Tornado," "Red Rock," "Crooked Nose," and "Bodacious" are now in the Hall of Fame. More recently, with the professional bull tour being such a success all over North America, an entirely new generation of top-notch bulls has emerged. Among the real fans of the bull tour, the bulls seem to be just about as well known as the bull riders. Dan Halpern, in an article in *The New York Times* magazine, reported that the OLN channel broadcast an hour-long biography of "Bodacious,"

Guy Weeks on Big John   Denver '64

bulls. . . . Now we have bull rankings and statistics and bull profiles" in the broadcast of the BPR events.

And the bulls in all types of rodeo competition are tough. The 2005 PRCA Bull of the Year, "War Dance," owned by Harry Vold's Broken Arrow Rodeos, had been ridden only once in the past three years. That is just one example of how challenging these bulls have become. The National Finals Rodeo bulls are selected by the

top bull riders, so the selection is taken as a very serious choice by guys who ride these hurricanes all year long. It is unheard of for a bull rider at the NFR to make a qualified ride for ten straight performances. The bulls are too violent, and after a few performances the cowboy's body begins to break down. It's a good day for the bull riders when they manage to stay aboard for the eight-second ride 50 percent of the time.

It is not uncommon among real rodeo followers to come to a particular rodeo just to see one of these famous horses or bulls and to see how the cowboys would meet the challenge that the fans knew they would face. It would be hard to calculate the number of fans who bought tickets to a rodeo to see Charmayne James run the barrels on "Scamper," himself a Hall of Fame inductee. But because there are so many stock contractors breeding animals just for the rodeo arena, there is certainly no shortage of tough bulls and horses. Watching the Professional Bull Riders (PBR) tour on TV, the viewer immediately senses that the sport has emerged as a classic duel between cowboy and animal, with the bulls regularly beating the cowboys. And as if to rub it in, the information about the bulls shown on TV is often more complete than the data about the rider. You wonder who the stars really are!

Insurance ✦ On a more practical note, in 1951, a blanket insurance policy had been written for RCA members, and although the initial $5 dues had to be upped to $25 (of which $20 went to covering the insurance premium), the cowboys were happy to have the coverage. For the dues-paying cowboys, their coverage included

ABOVE: Bill Kornell aboard Summit Rodeo Company's bull #469 "Jet Age" at the 1967 National Finals Rodeo in Oklahoma City. Photo courtesy of the Professional Rodeo Cowboys Association.

going to and from the rodeo as well as the time they were actually competing in the arena. But this wasn't always the way the cowboys felt about being part of an entity that was bigger than they were. In 1946, writing for

It is not uncommon among real rodeo followers to come to a particular rodeo just to see one of these famous horses or bulls.

Western Horseman, Jerry Armstrong reported that "the insurance coverage for rodeo contestants scheduled to go into effect this season has failed to materialize. Earl Lindsey, the very efficient R.C.A. manager, worked hard to put the insurance plan over. . . . The catch was that Manager Lindsey had to secure at least 100 paid members at six dollars each by Jan. 1 before the insurance company would issue the policy. There are some 1,500 R.C.A. members and only 86 of them had subscribed by the deadline. This policy was for a year and covered any accident in the arena." It took five more years for the cowboys to accept the kind of coverage that has become such an important part of their careers.

Rodeo Sports News ✦ As rodeo continued to grow, cowboys, cowgirls, horses, and bulls all gained in popularity, and the RCA, in November 1952, decided to enter into some new territory—namely, the publication of their own newspaper, *The Rodeo Sports News.* In February 1953, the newspaper was named the official publication of the RCA. The paper gave the cowboys all the information that they needed about future RCA-approved rodeos, rodeo results, feature articles, and even bits and pieces of rodeo news. Television coverage was becoming more prominent, and in 1957 *The Rodeo Sports News* reported that tens of millions watched the one-hour coverage of the Pendleton Round-Up on 168 CBS stations. This was the first time television covered an outdoor rodeo.

The National
Finals

Wayne Robinson bulldogging at Jackson, Mississippi, in 1969. The hazer is unidentified. Courtesy of the Professional Rodeo Cowboys Association.

Rodeo

The NFR selected 210 saddle broncs, bareback horses, and bulls, with another 40 in reserve. During the year, the stock contractors were told to keep accurate records of their rough stock so when the final decisions were made, the best stock would be in Dallas. They had to keep records of where each horse or bull **rider** was bucked, what they scored, who the rider was, how they were rated, and all such data. In the final count, twenty-five different stock contractors were represented at the NFR.

The winners of the first National Finals averages (not necessarily the year-long winners) were the following:

Saddle Bronc: Jim Tescher, Medora, South Dakota
Bareback Riding: Jack Buschbom, Mobridge,
     South Dakota
Steer Wrestling: Willard Combs, Checotah, Oklahoma
Team Roping: Jim Rodriquez Jr. and Gene Rambo,
     both from California
Calf Roping: Olin Young, Albuquerque, New Mexico
Bull Riding: Jim Shoulders, Henryetta, Oklahoma.

Shoulders also won the All-Around buckle. Everett Shaw of Stonewall, Oklahoma, was declared steer-roping champion for the year. Jane Mayo was the top barrel racer.

The NFR was now a major event for rodeo, and some of the best people in the Rodeo Cowboys Association were in charge of making sure that everything went smoothly. Montanan Bill Linderman was the arena director; Buster Ivory of Pampa, Texas, was the Livestock Superintendent; two other Montanans, Cy Taillon and Pete Logan, were the announcers; and D. J Gaudin, Buck LeGrand, and Gene Clark were the bullfighters/clowns. "Trails End," owned by Oral Zumwalt, was selected as

Maybe the biggest groundbreaking decision in rodeo was the decision to hold a national finals rodeo—a World Series or Super Bowl for cowboys and eventually for barrel racers.

The idea for a National Finals Rodeo (NFR) had been under discussion for several years during the 1950s, and a commission, headed by John Van Cronkhite, was even assembled to formulate the plans and select a location. One hundred and twenty-five cities were asked to submit plans, and eventually the committee narrowed down their choices to Dallas, Texas; Los Angeles, California; and Louisville, Kentucky. They ultimately selected Dallas, with the city of Dallas and the Texas State Fair as the sponsors. Finally, in 1959, with CBS prepared to televise the event, the first National Finals Rodeo was held in the 8,000-seat Livestock Coliseum in Dallas from December 26 to 30. It was also decided to hold the National Finals Steer Roping in Clayton, on the north eastern plains of New Mexico, partially because a much bigger arena was needed for this event.

the top saddle bronc; "Old Speck," owned by Beutler Bros. and Son, topped the bulls; and Harry Knight's "Come Apart" was the number-one bareback horse.

The National Finals became a big draw and the cowboys—and eventually the cowgirls—competed all year to make the end-of-the-year championships. The top fifteen contestants in each event are now invited, and they compete for more money in the ten days of competition than they would see in any one rodeo during the rest of the year. In 1959, the prize money at finals was $50,000, and by 2004, the total prize money for the NFR had been upped to nearly $5,100,000. In 1959, Jim Shoulders earned $32,905 for the entire year as All-Around Cowboy. In 2005, Ryan Jarrett of Summerville, Georgia, took home $263,665 for the same crown. In 1959, saddle bronc champion Casey Tibbs of Fort Pierre, South Dakota, finished the year with total winnings of $17,485. Jeffery Willert of Belvedere, South Dakota, the 2005 World Champion Saddle Bronc rider, took home $278,169.

Rodeo was certainly moving in the right direction, and in 1959 the NFR gave it another push along the same lines. The five-day competition in Dallas was a success, but it had always been the intention of the National Finals Rodeo Commission to hold the rodeo in a new location every three years. The original plan was for rodeo to gain more recognition throughout the country, as the competition moved around, and hopefully new fans would be won over.

For the next three-year cycle, 1962 to 1964, the Los Angeles Sports Arena was selected. The Finals were also a success there—the money was even upped from $50,000 to $60,000—but problems arose that were never faced in Dallas. First and foremost, the city of Los Angeles was not nearly as committed to the cowboy lifestyle as the Texans were, and the 1963 Finals were scheduled to start just after President John F. Kennedy was assassinated. The attendance was ultimately down during the three years in Los Angeles, but there were some very positive strides made because television ratings were good and for the first time California sports

ABOVE: George Myren, a 2004 inductee into the Canadian Professional Rodeo Hall of Fame, on Zumwalt's "Fox" at Billings, Montana, 1957. Courtesy of George Myren.

RIGHT: Rodeo clown working a Harper & Morgan Rodeo Company bull at the National Finals Rodeo. Photo by Brenda Allen, courtesy of the Professional Rodeo Cowboys Association.

writers actually devoted time and column space to rodeo.

The next three-year segment took the NFR back to cowboy country, to Oklahoma City at the Jim Norick Arena. That was the same year the National Cowboy Hall of Fame and Western Heritage Center in Oklahoma City was dedicated. This museum has continued to grow and today is one of the leading centers for the preservation of western and rodeo history and culture. The National Cowboy Hall of Fame has expanded and now houses an especially significant rodeo photographic archive.

Tom Bews on Blue Sage - Medicine Hat Stampede - July 27-1967 - Kesler Stock

As it turned out, Oklahoma City wound up hosting the National Finals Rodeo from 1965 through 1984, way beyond the original three-year limit. The National Finals Rodeo and Oklahoma City just seemed to be a good fit. The attendance significantly increased each year, with the nine-performance rodeo growing from 47,027 fans in 1965 to 89,200 in 1974, the last year before the event was expanded to ten performances. By the time it was set at ten performances (the present format), the rodeo had moved to the Myriad

LEFT: Canadian Tom Bews on Kesler's saddle bronc "Blue Sage" at the Medicine Hat Stampede in Alberta in 1967. Photo by Fred Kobsted, courtesy of the Professional Rodeo Cowboys Association.

Arena, and the sold-out attendance was 117,070. The prize money shot up from $44,500 in 1965 to $121,500 in 1975, and with ten performances the prize money in 1984 was $901,550. But maybe the most important thing for the cowboys was that Oklahoma City, as a city, seemed totally committed to the event and really laid out the red carpet for the cowboys.

By this time team roping had been brought into the regular National Finals—it started out as a separate event along with steer roping but moved to Scottsdale, Arizona, and then to Santa Maria, California, before it joined the big show in 1963. Steer roping remained apart from the main rodeo, moving from its first year in Clayton, New Mexico, on a journey that took it to several places, including a one-year stay in Laramie, Wyoming (1961), then a return from 1973 to 1983, then to Guthrie, Oklahoma, from 1984 to 2000, and more recently, Amarillo, Texas, starting there in 2001. Fortunately for the steer ropers, their prize money has grown as well. It has gone from a modest $5,000 in 1959 to a more challenging $121,251 in 2004. In 1959, the champion steer roper, Everett Shaw of Stonewall, Oklahoma, won $5,155. In 2005, champion steer roper, Scott Snedecor of Uvalde, Texas, finished the year with a take of $69,382, beating out eighteen-time world champion Guy Allen of Santa Anna, Texas, in the closest championship contest ever held. He won by a mere $1.67.

ABOVE: All-Around cowboy and legendary bull rider, Freckles Brown, riding Steiner's bull #67 at the Waco, Texas, Fair and Rodeo in 1961. Photo by Ferrell Butler, courtesy of the Professional Rodeo Cowboys Association.

RIGHT: Dave Shields on the bareback horse "Tailor Made" at Estevan, Saskatchewan, Canada, in 1984. Photo by Cobbe, courtesy of the Professional Rodeo Cowboy Association.

Canadian Professional Rodeo Association ❖

The Canadian Professional Rodeo Association got on board in 1974 when they started their own Finals, and it has been as big a success in Canada as the American NFR has been in the States. From 1974 through 2004, Canadian attendance increased from a first-year total of 24,499 fans to a packed house of 94,233 in Edmonton, Alberta. The purse increased from $29,478 to $1,020,000. The Canadians hold their rodeo in mid-November because many of the Canadians also qualify for the PRCA Finals in December. The Canadians are proud of their "strong working relationship with the PRCA . . . and Canadian professional rodeos are co-approved for World championships." The American NFR has always been considered the World Championship.

The Canadians were a little slower in getting rodeo organized into a professional association than the Americans. In 1944, Ken Thomson, on a weekend pass from the air force, and Arnold Montgomery, an all-event contestant

from Drumheller, Alberta, got a group of cowboys together in Vancouver, British Columbia. Their only goal was to create an insurance fund for injured cowboys.

A month later, at the Calgary Stampede, the Cowboys' Insurance Association was started with each contestant contributing a dollar at each rodeo entered. That sum was to be matched by the rodeo committees.

ABOVE: World Champion bull rider Freckles Brown of Lawton, Oklahoma, on #554 during the first go-round at Cheyenne, 1960. Notice the bull fighter moving in to protect the rider if he should hit the ground. Photo by Devere, courtesy of the Professional Rodeo Cowboys Association.

LEFT: Royce Smith of Challis, Idaho, on a bareback horse at Kissimmee, Florida, in 1975. Smith finished ranked fifth in the world for the year. Photo courtesy of the Professional Rodeo Cowboy Association.

OPPOSITE: The "Rodeo Ballet." Contestants stretching behind the chutes before their event. Photo courtesy of Louise L. Serpa, Tucson, Arizona.

Art Johnson trailing bucking horses to the Calgary Stampede circa 1930s. Photo courtesy of the Professional Rodeo Cowboys Association.

The next year, 1945, once again at the Calgary Stampede, the cowboys renamed their organization the Cowboys' Protective Association (CPA), and they quickly adopted three rules:

1. Every rodeo would guarantee a minimum purse of $100 per event.
2. Contestants' entry fees must be added to the purse.
3. Judges would be appointed by the association.

Up until this meeting, many rodeos in Canada paid out as little as $10 for first place, entry fees were not part of the purse, and judging was done by amateurs or men who had never ridden rough stock or roped a calf or steer. These conditions were very similar to those that caused the formation of the Cowboys' Turtle Association nearly ten years earlier in the United States.

In addition, the Canadians established that stock would be selected by a draw, a go-round formula became part of the rodeo, the pick-up men were also to assist bareback riders—not just saddle bronc riders, and bullfighters were going to be used to aid the bull riders getting off their animals.

There were twenty-six rodeos during the first year of the CPA with All-Around Cowboy Carl Olson earning $1,221. By 2004, there were fifty-eight sanctioned rodeos, and All-Around Cowboy Rod Warren took home $44,640.

ABOVE: Joe Alexander, the most dominant bareback rider of the 1970s, on a ride in 1975. Alexander shares the record for most bareback titles (five) with Bruce Ford and holds the record for the most consecutive titles (five), 1971–75. Photo by Gustafson Rodeo Photography, courtesy of Joe Alexander.

The cowboys of the Canadian Professional Rodeo Association are all eligible to join the PRCA and compete on the American circuit, and many do extremely well.

Over the years the Canadians have produced some of the very best rough stock riders, including Jerry Ambler, Winston Bruce, Kenny McLean, Marty Wood, Wayne Vold, Mel Hyland, Ivan Daines, Mel Coleman, Rod Hay, Denny Hay, Glen O'Neill, and Rod Warren. Add to this list Dale Trottier, Robin Burwash, Steve Dunham, and

Jim Dunn. These are all saddle bronc and bareback riders who have not only starred on the Canadian circuit but have also been major figures in the PRCA rodeos. And Jim Gladstone, of Cardston, Alberta, won the most money at the NFR in 1977 in calf roping, the only Canadian to ever rank that high in that event. In 2005, Lee Graves of Calgary, the five-time Canadian Steer Wrestling Champion, became the World Steer Wrestling Champion as he crushed the opposition in Las Vegas by placing in nine of the ten go-rounds, setting a record for the most money won at a single rodeo, $126,415. For the year, he earned $206,415.

Of all the recognition that the Canadians have received, particularly in the States, they have received some of their highest accolades for their rough stock—their bucking horses. The late Reg Kesler, Vold Rodeo, Calgary Stampede, Kesler Rodeo Co. (Reg's son Greg), Franklin Rodeo Company, and Kesler Championship Rodeo (Reg's grandson Duane) have all contributed championship horses to rodeos in Canada and the United States. At the 2005 NFR, one of the TV announcers described the Kesler stock as "big, strong, and not tame in the chutes." It is not uncommon to find horses owned by Canadian stock contractors selected by the cowboys as "Horse of the Year" for the regular season and at the NFR. Those Canadian horses come from rough country.

The Canadian Professional Rodeo Association turned into a major success story, and they now sanction over sixty rodeos a year in the four western provinces with a total purse of well over $5 million. They have a membership of nearly 800 with an additional 735 permit holders. They are also an "umbrella" group, just like the PRCA, that in addition to the contestants, committees and stock contractors, timers, judges, associate members, announcers, bullfighters, photographers, rodeo secretaries, and specialty act performers are all headquartered in Calgary.

More

Three cowboys wearing their woolies, waiting to enter the arena, c. 1910.

Changes

Back in the United States, the National Finals Rodeo was a resounding triumph and both attendance and purse money for the entire year was increasing. The total payout for 1953 was $2,492,856, and by 1984 (the NFR's last year in Oklahoma City), the yearly total for all approved rodeos had grown to $13,776,848.

The Move to Las Vegas

If things were going so well, why did the NFR leave Oklahoma City? There are several stories and anyone can rationalize any way they want to about what caused the change of locale, but ultimately it was about money and growth. There was a feeling that Oklahoma City had reached its limits and that they were essentially locked into what they were already doing with very little potential for any more expansion. In addition, Benny Binion, who owned a casino in Las Vegas and was always a friend of the cowboys, joined in a push to bring the NFR to the city in southern Nevada. As part of his pitch, he also made a promise to increase the prize money. Binion felt that Las Vegas could offer his cowboy friends more advantages than Oklahoma City could—especially prize money, hotel accommodations, food, and entertainment. In fact, Benny wanted the cowboys and their families to have a "good time." In the first years of the NFR in Las Vegas, Benny Binion paid every contestant's NFR entry fees. Though he had never competed in the rodeo arena, Binion had been a rancher and a horseman, roping colts for branding each year. Past and present stock contractors have always commented that Binion raised some of the best bucking horses, pickup horses, and saddle horses that rodeo had ever seen. In 1985, the year the NFR left Oklahoma City and moved to Las Vegas, Benny Binion was named ProRodeo's Man of the Year, an award presented each year by the Professional Rodeo Cowboys Association. In 1988, Binion was inducted into the ProRodeo Hall of Fame under the category of Notables.

Binion's plans, however, did not just sail through the PRCA Board. After some very contentious board meetings, the vote was taken, and except for a nay vote from the stock contractor and former contestant Reg Kesler, the move to Las Vegas was approved. Kesler, with ranches located in Alberta, Canada, and Missoula, Montana, just didn't think it was the right thing to do to Oklahoma City. He believed that Oklahoma City had given the Finals a major role in rodeo and had brought stability to it. In his opinion, it wasn't a very loyal way for the PRCA to act. Kesler made it clear that he didn't think "it was the cowboy way." But the move did take place, and ultimately it has proven to be an enormous success for both Las Vegas and the PRCA, although Oklahoma City proved to be the odd man out.

Early December, the time of the National Finals Rodeo, had always been considered a "slack" period in Las Vegas. It was sort of between seasons or between events—between Thanksgiving and Christmas. When the NFR settled into Las Vegas, that all changed. The rodeo people came in crowds, they shopped and filled hotel rooms and restaurants and left lots of money in the casinos. In return, the rodeo crowd was treated well by the city.

ABOVE: Shawn Davis with Benny Binion in Las Vegas in 1985. Binion was one of the major movers in bringing the NFR to Las Vegas. Photo courtesy of Shawn Davis.

It wasn't long before the prize money ballooned to a size none of the cowboys or even the PRCA ever envisioned, and there was some serious talk about building a separate arena just for the rodeo. That hasn't happened yet and the Finals are still held at the Thomas & Mack Center of the University of Nevada at Las Vegas (UNLV), an arena that many of the cowboys feel is too small, particularly for the ropers and barrel racers.

The National Finals Rodeo has been sold out for seventeen straight years and in 2003 set a record of 176,625 people for the ten-day event. In that same year, they also set a single day's record of 18,104 screaming, cheering, enthusiastic fans.

After the 2005 Finals, it was announced that the PRCA and Las Vegas had extended their agreement so that the National Finals Rodeo will remain in the desert city at least through 2014.

Rodeo as a Professional Sport

Rodeo had been accepted as a professional sport long before the Finals in Las Vegas. In 1964, the RCA had moved to larger and more centrally located headquarters in Denver, and in 1966 the *Denver Post* announced that they would report rodeo results on the sports page. This may seem like a minor declaration but it was a goal that the RCA had been aiming at for many years. This was a serious announcement that rodeo was, in fact, a professional sport.

In some ways this idea of professionalism has to be clarified. If a professional athlete is defined as an athlete who competes for money, then there is no problem. But as Americans understand professional sports, rodeo is quite a bit different. First, there is no sense of team or team organization. There aren't any team planes, buses, agents, or personal PR people. Rodeo is an individual sport. The cowboys and cowgirls don't travel with coaches, and they select what rodeos they choose to enter and when and if they want to take time off. Rodeo cowboys pay an entry fee each time they compete, and that can amount to hundreds of dollars per rodeo with no guarantees that the contestant would recover any of that money. They also pay dues to the Professional Rodeo Cowboys Association for the privilege to compete. And what makes rodeo such a tough way to earn a living, particularly in this age of high-cost travel and lodging, is there are no guarantees, no appearance money, no promised salaries, and no long-term deals. If you win, you win, but if you don't place, you go home empty-handed and are out your travel expenses and entry fee.

During the period of the 1950s through the 1970s, champions like Casey Tibbs of Fort Pierre, South Dakota; Deb Copenhaver of Post Falls, Idaho; Shawn Davis of Whitehall, Montana; Guy Weeks of Abilene, Texas; Enoch Walker and Bill Smith of Cody, Wyoming; Alvin Nelson of Sentinel Butte, South Dakota; and Dennis Reiners of Clara City, Minnesota, emerged as just a few of the top saddle bronc riders of their era. Jim Shoulders of Henryetta, Oklahoma; Harry Tompkins of Dublin,

ABOVE: John Edwards, originally from the East, became a top-flight bareback rider, including many trips to the NFR. Here he is on Vold's "Old Yeller." Wayne Vold is the pickup man in this 1971 action shot from Kennewick, Washington. Photo by Fred Kobsted. Courtesy of the Professional Rodeo Cowboys Association.

RIGHT: Charley Roe is dogging while "Smiley" Adams hazes in Illinois, 1972. Photo by Bern Gregory, courtesy of the Professional Rodeo Cowboys Association.

In recent years corporate sponsorships have made it easier for the top echelon of cowboys to cover their expenses, especially if they are injured and can't compete—and for rodeo cowboys, if you don't compete, there is no way to earn any money, although recently rodeo has generated product endorsements for many of the top hands.

The RCA Logo ❖ The 1960s was also the period when the RCA adopted their logo, taken from a photograph by one of the very best of the rodeo photographers, DeVere Helfrich. His picture of Bill Ward on the bronc "Sea Lion" was taken in 1956 at the San Angelo, Texas, Stock Show and Rodeo, and that logo is the one still in use today and is displayed proudly on pickup truck windows and a variety of merchandise. Helfrich was sure that the best time to take a picture of a bronc rider was when the cowboy's feet were forward and the horse's hooves were just about to hit the ground. This concept is what made the shot of Bill Ward such a classic.

Helfrich was a pioneering rodeo photographer and was one of the trio that many fans refer to as "the big three"—Ralph Russell Doubleday, John Addison Stryker, and John DeVere Helfrich.

Fortunately for rodeo, in these couple of decades the rodeo cowboys began to gain some of the same popularity and fame that athletes in other sports had already achieved. Certainly not to the same degree, but there was more and more coverage in the sports pages, and the RCA did a much better job of promoting the sport

LEFT: The ProRodeo Hall of Fame in Colorado Springs, Colorado, was dedicated in 1979. Out front is the statue of Casey Tibbs, the great saddle bronc rider. Initially the Board of Trustees was made up of some of the giants of rodeo: Joe Alexander, Hugh Bennett, Freckles Brown, Shawn Davis, Ben Johnson, Harry Knight, Larry Mahan, Harley May, Dean Oliver, Slim Pickens, Everett Shaw, and Jim Shoulders are just a few of the rodeo stars on the board. Photo courtesy of the Professional Rodeo Cowboys Association.

BELOW: Dave Maddox on Stephens Brothers' bull, #44 "Kingman Copenhagen" at Pendleton in 1989. Photo courtesy of the Professional Rodeo Cowboys Association.

Texas; Benny Reynolds of Melrose, Montana; Dean Oliver of Boise, Idaho; and Larry Mahan, of Brooks, Oregon, surfaced as All-Around champions and showed their athletic ability in more than one event. This was also the era when Jim Houston of Omaha, Nebraska; Jack Buschbom of Cassville, Wisconsin; Ralph Buell of Sheridan, Wyoming; Bruce Ford of Evans, Colorado; and Joe Alexander of tiny Cora, Wyoming, dominated the bareback riding as much as Dean Oliver. Glen Franklin of House, New Mexico; Olin Young of Peralta, New Mexico; and Ronnye Sewalt of Chico, Texas, were among the most dominant calf ropers. In the period well before the Professional Bull Riders (PBR) tour was organized, Jim Shoulders, Freckles Brown of Soper, Oklahoma; Ronnie Rossen, of Broadus, Montana; Larry Mahan, Myrtis Dightman of Houston, Texas; Don Gay from Mesquite, Texas; and Bill Kornell, out of Chico, Texas, were just a few of the major names in the bull riding competition.

and the cowboys to the general public. Even corporate America joined the rodeo parade as corporate sponsorships began to play a more prominent role.

In 1975, the RCA placed the word *professional* in front of their name to become the Professional Rodeo Cowboys Association (PRCA). Some claim that it was done to solidify the "professional" and that it was "a more accurate name for what had become the largest and most prestigious sanctioning body in the history of rodeo." Others argue that the name change was forced by RCA, the electronics giant, who was claiming some sort of copyright infringement. For whatever reason, the name change was made, and just a few years later, in 1979, the entire organization moved again, this time about sixty miles south to a new facility on the north end of Colorado Springs. With this change came the addition of the long-awaited ProRodeo Cowboy Hall of Fame, which has become a very popular tourist attraction and a depository for a host of rodeo records, artifacts, and quite a few pieces of high-quality sculpture.

LEFT: Billy Kiche on Bar T Inc.'s bareback horse "Born Free" at Evanston, Wyoming, in 1995. Photo courtesy of the Professional Rodeo Cowboys Association.

BELOW: Canadian Jerry Ambler, one of the smoothest saddle bronc riders and 1946 World Champion, on "Water Smyth" at Sheridan, Wyoming, in 1935.

OPPOSITE: Stock Contractor Steve Sutton of South Dakota serving as a pickup man during the 1995 NFR. Photo by Dan Hubbell, courtesy of the Professional Rodeo Cowboys Association.

ABOVE: Unidentified cowboy being bucked off Alsbaugh's "Beverly" at the 1982 Boulder Pow-Wow. Photo by C & B Moore, courtesy of Professional Rodeo Cowboys Association.

BELOW, LEFT: Mark Garrett on #207 "Skoals Instant Request" from the Kesler Rodeo Company at the 1994 NFR. Mark's brother, Marvin, was the 1994 World Champion bareback rider. The cowboys are from South Dakota. Photo by Andy Watson, courtesy of the Professional Rodeo Cowboys Association.

BELOW, RIGHT: Former college champion (1975) at Montana State University and many times NFR saddle bronc rider, Bud Monroe, at Cheyenne in 1984. Photo by Jan Spencer, courtesy of the Professional Rodeo Cowboys Association.

RCA Presidents ⚜ After Toots Mansfield resigned from the presidency of the RCA in 1951, another rodeo legend took over. Bill Linderman, who was a champion All-Around Cowboy three times, Saddle Bronc Champion twice, and Bareback Champion and Steer Wrestling Champion during his career, moved up from the vice presidency to assume the RCA leadership. Linderman was so well regarded by his fellow cowboys that he was known as "The King," and many still believe that he was the greatest cowboy who ever competed. He was often described as someone who looked like a cowboy should.

Linderman, one of five brothers from Montana, was a natural leader. His first elected position within the RCA was as bareback bronc riding representative on the board of directors. He served as president from 1951 until 1957. From 1962 until his death in 1965, he was the RCA secretary-treasurer.

ABOVE: Dale Smith, a former president of the RCA, with his horse "Poker Chip." Smith was inducted into the ProRodeo Hall of Fame as a team roper in 1979. Photo courtesy of the Professional Rodeo Cowboys Association.

In one of those tragic events that can't ever be explained, Linderman was on his way to meet with officials from the Northwest Washington Fair and Rodeo at Puyallup when the commercial airliner that he was flying on crashed and burned in Salt Lake City on November 11, 1965, killing forty-one people, including "The King."

During Linderman's tenure as RCA president, the insurance program was initiated and the *Rodeo Sports News* was started with Gene Lamb as editor. Linderman refused a seventh term as president in 1957 and was succeeded in office by Harley May, who served from 1957 to 1959. May was one of the first college champions to become an outstanding pro; he was a World Champion steer wrestler several times over and was in office when the National Finals Rodeo was inaugurated.

In 1960, Jack Buschbom, one of the great bareback riders of his era, was elected president. A native of Wisconsin, Jack's father was a former bronc rider and stock contractor. Buschbom won the World Championship in bareback riding in 1949, 1959, and 1969 and never finished below fourth in the standings during his entire fourteen-year career.

In 1961, Dale Smith, a team roper from Chandler, Arizona, took over the presidency and served for seventeen years in a job that still paid no salary. In addition to being a team roper, Smith also roped calves and steers and made the finals in each event. During his terms in office, the headquarters of the RCA were moved to Denver and the scoring system in use today—based on the 100 total—was put into place. The scoring system is easy to understand. Each of the two judges is responsible for 50 points and awards a score of 1 to 25 for the rider and 1 to 25 for the bull or horse. The combined scores of the two judges, if everything is perfect—and that has happened only once—would total 100. In 1991, Wade Leslie rode "Wolfman," a bull owned by the Growney Brothers Rodeo Company from Red Bluff, California, to this perfect score at a rodeo in Central Point, Oregon.

When Dale Smith lost the election in 1970 (he was reelected in 1971), Clem McSpadden took over. He was a Native American, who during his professional career

Ragsdale had been to the National Finals Rodeo in calf roping from 1961 until 1975 and was runner-up to the All-Around in 1972.

Bob Ragsdale, former PRCA president and All-Around Cowboy competitor, wrestling a steer at Clovis, California, in 1963. Photo by Ben Allen, courtesy of the Professional Rodeo Cowboys Association.

was an Oklahoma rancher, state senator, U.S. Congressman, and RCA announcer. He was also selected to be the first American announcer at the Calgary Stampede and the Canadian Finals Rodeo. McSpadden had been on the board of directors of the RCA for some years and was an articulate spokesman for rodeo.

In 1973, Dale Smith again lost the presidency, this time to the calf roper and steer wrestler Bob Ragsdale of Chowchilla, California. Ragsdale had been to the National Finals Rodeo in calf roping from 1961 until 1975 and was runner-up to the All-Around in 1972. His

term was for two years. In 1976, Dale Smith took back the presidency and served until the end of 1981. During Smith's last term the PRCA left Denver and moved to their new site on the north edge of Colorado Springs.

Shawn Davis, originally from Whitehall, Montana, became the new president in 1982. One of the great saddle bronc riders of his era, Davis won the World Championship in 1965, 1967, and 1968. He had previously been on the Board of Directors as the saddle bronc director. Davis competed in an era that produced some of the very best post–World War II saddle bronc riders. That list included Bill Smith, Enoch Walker, Winston

Bruce, Guy Weeks, Jim Tescher, Marty Wood, Dennis Reiners, Hugh Chambliss, Mel Hyland, Tom Bews, and a host of others. His accomplishments in the arena against that level of competition are quite remarkable.

After retiring from his riding career, Shawn Davis served as co-general manager of the National Finals Rodeo with John Burke of Casper, Wyoming, from 1986 to 1991, and in 1992 he was appointed as the sole general

BELOW: This is a Hamley saddle that the World Champion Saddle Bronc rider of 1946, Jerry Ambler, purchased in 1941. After his death in 1958, the saddle eventually wound up in the hands of Bill Smith, who used it to become World Champion Saddle Bronc rider in 1969, 1971, and 1973. Today the saddle is in the ProRodeo Hall of Fame as part of the Bill Smith exhibition. Photo courtesy of the ProRodeo Hall of Fame.

manager, a job he continues to hold. Today Davis is the coach of the Southern Idaho College rodeo team where he has recently been inducted into their Hall of Fame. He was elected to the ProRodeo Hall of Fame in 1979.

Following Shawn Davis to the presidency was Dan Taylor of Doole, Texas. Taylor was a former calf roper and in 1942 became a member of the Cowboys' Turtle Association. During his term in office the PRCA adopted the new automatic barriers for the roping events, brought to the PRCA by two Texans—Elton Allen and Claude Mullins.

Despite a long and distinguished career in all aspects of rodeo, Dan Taylor was removed from office by the PRCA members late in 1986. His disagreement with the other cowboys was over when and where members could compete. He felt that outsiders, mostly the sponsors, were interfering too often in the decisions that the PRCA was making.

T. J. Walters, a Texan and twelve-time NFR bareback contestant during the 1970s and early 1980s, took over the presidency and served through 1987 when the PRCA hired their first commissioner.

Weekend Warriors ✦ In 1975, the RCA made a big change about how the pro circuit would be run and how to accommodate all the cowboys and cowgirls who didn't "go down the road" full time. That year the governing

LANE FROST #171 (Burns) PRO-TOUR CASPER '85 "MR.T"

LEFT: Lane Frost on Pete Burn's bull #171 "Mr. T" at Casper, Wyoming, in 1985. Frost was the World Champion bull rider in 1987 and was tragically gored to death by a bull at Cheyenne in 1989. He was 25 years old. The film *8 Seconds* is the story of Frost's life that was cut short by a cross-bred bull called "Bad-to-the-Bone." Lane Frost was inducted into the ProRodeo Hall of Fame in 1990. Photo by Fain, courtesy of the Professional Rodeo Cowboys Association.

These are the people that typically work regular jobs during the week and then when the weekend arrives, they hit the rodeo road, usually staying fairly close to home.

Great Lakes, and Southeastern circuits, all established to make room for part-time cowboys and cowgirls. These are the people that typically work regular jobs during the week and then when the weekend arrives, they hit the rodeo road, usually staying fairly close to home. The reasons why this happens are wide ranging, but for most of people, their families and jobs or businesses keep them tied to a very specific geographic area and prevent them from traveling full time.

In an article for *American Profile*, Tracy Leinberger-Leonardi interviewed several of these "weekend warriors," and they all agree that the circuit system has allowed them to participate in rodeo and that without it they would have had to drop out. Ann Bleiker, senior public relations coordinator for the PRCA says, "The weekend warrior doesn't want to spend 365 days a year

body of pro rodeo took into account the fact that not all rodeo cowboys could be on the circuit full time and decided to do something to keep the "weekend warriors" as active competitors by creating the circuit system. The country was divided into twelve regions. California, Texas, and Montana each made up one region. A few regions included two states, like the Turquoise Circuit (New Mexico and Arizona) and the Columbia River Circuit (Washington and Oregon). The largest region was the First Frontier Circuit with thirteen states that covers the northeastern part of the country. There are also the Wilderness, Mountain States, Badlands, Prairie,

ABOVE: Second generation college cowgirls (left to right), sisters Christi and Kelli Sultemeier, New Mexico; Molly Swanson Powell and Jody Petersen, Montana; and Cheyenne Wimberley, Texas. All competed on the Vernon College women's championship. The Sultemeiers' mother and Petersen's mother knew each other and both won All-Around championships 1969 and 1970. Powell had qualified several times for the NFR in barrel racing after winning the college barrel racing title in 1995. Photo © Sylvia Gann Mahoney, Vernon, TX.

RIGHT: Cade Swor, shown competing at the Vernon College rodeo in 2002, qualified for the 2005 National Finals Rodeo the second time, after winning the reserve national college rodeo championship in 2003 while competing for Vernon College. Photo © Sylvia Gann Mahoney, Vernon, TX.

each March in Pocatello, Idaho. The DNCFR has a purse of well over $400,000 that places it in the upper echelon of rodeos.

Although the circuit system was conceived to award the "weekend" cowboys and cowgirls, there is nothing that prevents the full-timers from taking a circuit crown, so names like Ty Murray, Dan Mortenson, Ryan Mapston, Deb Greenough, Kristie Peterson, Rod Lyman, Jake Barnes, Cody Ohl, Charmayne James, Josh O'Byrne, and Sherry Cervi appear on the circuit winner's list with some frequency. These multiple NFR contestants make certain that they enter enough circuit rodeos and win to take home their circuit's crown. This gives the part-timers a chance to compete against the best, and they generally hold their own. Over the years a look at the complete list of circuit winners produces the names of cowboys and cowgirls that never come close to making the NFR. Since its inception the circuit system has proven to be very popular with the contestants and very successful at the box office and the DNCFR.

on the road. They want to stay close to home. They want a chance at a full-time job. It has nothing to do with a lack of talent. It comes down to a matter of time."

At the beginning of the season, each of the cowboys and cowgirls chooses a home circuit, and they then compete for points earned within the circuit to qualify for that region's finals. They are still eligible to compete in rodeos outside their own region. After the twelve circuit finals are completed, the top regular-season contestants and the winners of the circuit finals qualify for the Dodge National Circuit Finals Rodeo (DNCFR) held

Shelly Mathews Barrel Racing Champ INFR 1990

PRCA Commissioners
✦ In 1988, the PRCA reorganized its management structure and hired Lewis Cryer as its first rodeo commissioner, although he had no rodeo background. For ten years he had been the commissioner of the Pacific Coast Athletic Conference and before that

LEFT: Shelly Mathews, the barrel racing champion at the 1990 Indian National Finals Rodeo. Photo by Fain, courtesy of the Indian National Finals Rodeo.

BELOW: Stock contractor Mel Potter, father of World Champion barrel racer Sherry Cervi, leads the bucking horses into the arena. Photo courtesy of the Professional Cowboys Association.

Pro Rodeo Judging System
✦ In 1982 the PRCA, in a decision that was intended to further promote professionalism, introduced the Pro Rodeo Judging System. This new setup consisted of full-time judges and a backup of judges in reserve. Previously, the contestants had judged. Usually a cowboy who had been injured or for whatever reason was sitting out a particular rodeo would take on the responsibility to judge.

The old system seemed to work but the professionalism that rodeo was achieving, and all the additional money that was now in the pot, forced the PRCA to bring professional judges to the sport, the same conditions that existed in all the other major professional leagues.

he was the associate athletic director at the University of Oregon. His administrative skills, however, were excellent and under his leadership rodeo was enabled to grow rapidly. He negotiated contracts with Las Vegas for the NFR, with the Lazy E Arena in Guthrie, Oklahoma, for the National Finals Steer Roping, a major television deal with ESPN, and he led the drive that got the National Finals Rodeo a special insert in *USA Today*. He managed a budget of over $20 million and a growing membership. When Cryer resigned at the end of 1998, most people associated with the PRCA considered it a great loss.

Cryer was followed into office on August 1, 1998, by Steven J. Hatchell. Hatchell also came from a university athletic background, including a term as the commissioner of the Southwest Conference and the Big 12 Conference. During his term of office, which lasted until January 2005, the PRCA continued its steady growth.

Troy Ellerman, a lawyer, is the third commissioner of the PRCA and the first with a rodeo background. He had been on the board as contract personnel director and had a rodeo career that went back more than thirty years. He earned his professional card when he was nine years old and competed as a bull rider and with a specialty act—he was a trick rider—and competed right on through college.

At the beginning of 2005, when Ellerman took over, the PRCA was carrying a debt of $3.6 million. Ellerman worked closely with PRCA Chairman of the Board Tom Feller, and by September of that year the PRCA had a positive balance of $500,000, a remarkable $4.1 million turnaround. Concessions had to be made by all of the PRCA's constituents, but as Ellerman explained, "That's a testament to our sponsors, contestants and stock contractors. They stepped up to the plate."

Rodeo had grown, and it was no longer possible to be both an active participant and a leader, as the first presidents had been. To compete and run the operation was just out of the question. Rodeo had gotten too big and too complicated and required a very serious, businesslike approach.

Rodeo

Today

Ty Murray was an outstanding bull rider, and he went on to be a founding member of the Professional Bull Riders (PBA). Here he is being thrown off "After the Whistle" after he made a qualifying ride to take second place at Yucson in 1995. Photo courtesy of Louise L. Serpa, Tucson, Arizona.

In today's rodeo, the sport has achieved a level of financial success and an acceptance from the public that would have been unheard of fifty or sixty years ago. The Wrangler National Finals Rodeo is a resounding triumph. The year-long circuit, together with its brother events in Canada, and the emergence of women as more than just barrel racers, has helped to spread rodeo to all corners of North America. The continued newspaper and magazine coverage and extensive and improving television programming seems to forecast good things for the future as well.

An additional feature for rodeo that didn't exist sixty years ago is the "farm" system that has become a major training ground for professional rodeo. The farm system is for the youngsters in rodeo. The Little Britches Rodeo, up through high school, and finally intercollegiate rodeo, all ensure that there is a good pipeline for future rough stock riders, ropers, and barrel racers. Virtually all the competitors at the National Finals, for example, have some college behind them and most of them attended school on a rodeo scholarship.

National Little Britches Rodeo ✦ The Little Britches rodeos (NLBRA) are the junior version of the Professional Rodeo Cowboys Association. They may be even less than the junior version. Still, they have around 220 sanctioned rodeos in 13 different states, engaging some 1,800 kids aged five to eighteen from nearly 30 states. And the organization is still growing. Rodeo is doing well from the pros right on down to this sort of entry-level affair that includes states from North Dakota to Louisiana and Nevada to Michigan. If there is anything like a "farm system" for rodeo, the National Little Britches Rodeo circuit surely has to be part of that system.

Headquartered at the Spencer Penrose Equestrian Center in Colorado Springs, Colorado, until November 2005, the NLRA had its start in 1952 when a group of rodeo fans held their first kids competition, called the Little Britches Rodeo, at the Arapahoe County Fairgrounds in Littleton, Colorado. Everyone seems to agree that it was a wonderful success.

It remained a single event until 1961 when a small convention was held in Denver with representatives from several states. They started a national youth association with headquarters in Denver. In 1982 they moved to Colorado Springs.

The mission statement of the National Little Britches Rodeo Association is clear. "It is a non-profit venture to build sound, healthy minds and bodies—to develop character, self-reliance and good sportsmanship through competition in the great sport of rodeo."

The NLBRA is still an amateur program; there are no cash awards. The kids compete for saddles, buckles, gift certificates, and, most importantly, college scholarships. Many of these kids get so good that they also win college rodeo scholarships. A significant number of top college rodeo contestants and pro champions had their first taste of rodeo competition at the Little Britches shows.

Each July the NLBRA holds its own national finals. All you have to do to get a feel for this is to imagine more than 700 kids, aged five to eighteen, bringing an additional 2,500 family members to your arena. You will have to find space for about 900 horses, all the additional rodeo stock like bulls, steers, goats, calves, and bucking horses, and determine what you want to do with all the horse trailers and trucks that brought all these people and animals. In November 2005, the NLBRA moved its finals to Pueblo, Colorado, about forty miles south on I-25, because they had outgrown the Penrose Center and there wasn't the money to expand the facility. The NLBRA still maintains its business offices in Colorado Springs.

The finals are divided into a variety of age groups and there are twenty-eight contested events. When it's all over the year's champions are crowned.

One more feature of the NLBRA finals—all week long there are seminars and clinics put on by the very best pros in each of the events. For the youngster, this may be the best part of the experience. They get a chance to learn directly from world champions, National Finals contestants, and others they have admired from afar.

American Junior Rodeo Association ✦ The American Junior Rodeo Association (AJRA) was founded in 1952 by Alvin G. Davis of Brownfield, Texas. Each year the AJRA awards around $120,000 worth of pay-off money, scholarships, trailers, saddles, buckles, and other gear at the AJRA Finals Rodeo. This youth rodeo association has been one of the few of these junior outfits to be recognized on a regular basis by the PRCA.

Several great PRCA champions have come from the ranks of the AJRA, including Roy Cooper, Jim Sharp, Tuff Hedeman, Trevor Brazile, and Cody Ohl.

Many of the kids who compete on this circuit come from second- and third-generation rodeo families and grow up with the sport. They are rodeo groupies as soon as they know what a rodeo is.

National High School Rodeo Association ✦ The National High School Rodeo Association (NHSRA) started back in 1947 at Halletsville, Texas. Although they weren't yet a formal organization, they actually held a state final that year with one hundred Texas high school cowboys and cowgirls participating. New

LEFT: Ty Murray is one of the greatest All-Around cowboys in the history of modern professional rodeo. He started young, riding steers in an American Junior Rodeo Association rodeo in Tucson, 1980. Photo courtesy of Louise L. Serpa, Tucson, Arizona.

Mexico followed Texas in 1948, and by 1949 Louisiana, Montana, and South Dakota all held state finals, and there was even a National Finals held in Halletsville with the various state champions competing.

The actual NHSRA was officially formed in 1951 and incorporated in 1961 when 20 states were involved, sending nearly 300 state champions to the National Finals.

National Intercollegiate Rodeo Association

The idea for college rodeo as a sport started back in 1949 when representatives from thirteen colleges met and adopted a set of bylaws and a constitution. The National Intercollegiate Rodeo Association (NIRA) was born; they actually held their first National Finals at the Cow Palace in San Francisco. The top teams were Sul Ross State College, Cal Poly, San Luis Obispo, the University of Wyoming, New Mexico A&M (now New Mexico State University), and the University of New Mexico.

College rodeo has expanded at virtually the same pace that the rest of the rodeo world has grown. From the original 13 schools, there are now 142 colleges and universities that participate with somewhere around 3,300 student members. However, the NIRA has a few kinks that have never been worked out. Almost none of the rodeo teams at the four-year schools are part of the athletic department the way the football or basketball teams are. Because the cowboys and cowgirls have to pay entry fees and they compete for prize money, the NCAA will have nothing to do with them. Their skill levels are often so high that many college rodeo athletes are also members of the PRCA or the WPA, sometimes competing at a college rodeo and a pro rodeo on the same weekend.

The NIRA Finals has never been considered an NCAA championship. Most rodeo teams at the four-year schools are either completely independent organizations or considered college clubs, and they compete equally against four-year and two-year colleges. These conditions can make raising money a tricky business for some of the teams. The teams at the four-year schools, particularly those in Division I, because they don't belong to the NCAA, rarely get significant money from the athletic budget. The two-year schools—and there are many of them—don't face these problems and often are the stars of their school's athletic programs.

It would be almost impossible to name all the great rodeo performers who started in college. Ty Murray, Tuff Hedeman, Dan Mortensen, Rachael Myllymaki, Chris LeDoux, Guy Allen, Trevor Brazile, Jesse Bail, Stran Smith, Rod Warren, Matt Austin, Kappy Allen, Molly Powell, Howard Harris, Shawn Davis, Joe Alexander, Phil Lyne, Jesse Bail, Lee Graves, Bud Monroe, Jimmie Gibbs Monroe, Matt Austin, Jerome Schneeberger, Trevor Knowles, and hundreds more are all former college rodeo competitors. Many of these competitors even started earlier, in Little Britches and junior high and high school rodeo.

From 1970 to 1996 the college finals were held in Bozeman, at Montana State University. In 1999, the competition was moved to Casper, Wyoming.

National Senior Pro Rodeo Association

✦ Like tennis, skiing, and other individual sports, a great many rodeo performers start at a very young age, often encouraged by parents, and continue through high school and college. The best actually make it to the pros. Then what? Not to be left out of the mix, there is actually a National Senior Pro Rodeo Association that has contestants forty years and older, divided in three age divisions: forty to

ABOVE: When Ty Murray was winning his record setting 7 All-Around titles, he won money in the three roughstock events. Here he is on a bareback horse at Tucson in 1995. Ty Murray was inducted into the ProRodeo Hall of Fame as an All-Around Cowboy in 2000. Photo courtesy of Louise L. Serpa, Tucson, Arizona.

Charlie Haeberle riding a bareback horse at a rodeo in Calgary in the early 1930s. Note the rope halter and the rope flank strap, neither used in modern bareback riding. Photo courtesy of the Professional Rodeo Cowboys Association.

As surprising as this may all seem, the Senior Circuit has well over 1,500 participants in the United States and Canada, competing in twenty states and three Canadian Provinces, at over seventy-five rodeos.

forty-nine years old, fifty to fifty-nine years old, and over sixty. They also have roping events for those sixty-eight and older. These senior cowboys and cowgirls compete in bareback riding, saddle bronc riding, bull riding, steer wrestling, team roping, calf roping, ladies barrel racing, and ribbon roping. Many of the competitors on this circuit are former RCA or PRCA World Champions, NFR qualifiers, and NFR Champions. As surprising as this may all seem, the Senior Circuit has well over 1,500 participants in the United States and Canada, competing in twenty states and three Canadian Provinces, at over seventy-five rodeos.

Sonny Stangle of New Underwood, South Dakota, contacted one of rodeo's all-time greats, Turk Greenough, who was then living in Las Vegas, Nevada, and in May 1979 they had a meeting in Denver. Besides those two, attending were Cal Wood of South Dakota, Stan and Doris McKillip of Nebraska, and Frank and Gay Holliday of Montana. Melvin Tindol of Texas and Jared Nesset of

ABOVE: Steer Wrestler Dick Rosenburg, with his brother Jim, hazing, at Coulee City, Washington in May 1967. Photo by Ray Brogan, courtesy of the Professional Rodeo Cowboys Association.

LEFT: Getting an early start. A young calf rider getting encouragement from his father. Photo courtesy of Louise L. Serpa, Tucson, Arizona.

Wyoming were unable to attend but were an integral part of the founding members of this organization. And unlike the Turtles who were "slow in organizing," the NOTRA decided to hold their first finals in October 1979. They got right to it.

Seven states were represented at the first Finals, with competitors coming from South Dakota, Nebraska, Montana, Kansas, Texas, Oklahoma, and Wyoming. Today the circuit has a total purse of well over $1,000,000 and a Finals held in Winnemucca, Nevada, before capacity crowds. Now you will also see cowboys and cowgirls coming from California; Utah; Oregon; New Mexico; Arizona; Idaho; Alberta, Canada; and other locations all over the West.

The poet Paul Zarzyski was certainly correct when he wrote the wonderful and prophetic poem *Ain't No Life After Rodeo*. It's a hard sport to give up, no matter how old you are.

BELOW: Joe Alexander, then of Cora, Wyoming, on a classic bareback ride in 1975. Alexander entered the ProRodeo Hall of Fame in 1979. Photo courtesy of Joe Alexander.

Dogtown Slim's bull "Sonora Red." Photo courtesy of the
Professional Rodeo Cowboys Association.

The

Events

All professional rodeos have a standard set of events with standard rules. For the PRCA-sponsored rodeos, the events are bareback riding, steer wrestling, team roping, saddle bronc riding, tie-down roping, bull riding, steer roping (although this event is not competed in at all rodeos), and ladies barrel racing. In the rough stock events there are at least two judges, and each judge is responsible for half of the score for each ride. There are at least two judges in the other events as well. The rules adopted by The Professional Rodeo Cowboys Association are the rules that are generally adopted by all the other rodeo associations. They have evolved over the years and seem to be fairly set in their present format.

The All-Around Cowboy, although not an event, is determined by the PRCA cowboy who wins the most prize money in a year while competing in at least two events, winning a minimum of $3,000 in each event. This cowboy is generally considered the most versatile cowboy in the sport. For example, Trevor Brazile of Decatur, Texas, the 2004 All-Around, earned nearly $254,000, with $119,696 coming in tie-down roping, $65,989 in team roping, and $67,921 in steer roping. The 2005 All-Around, Ryan Jarrett from Summerville, Georgia, took home $263,665. He won $105,042 in steer wrestling, $153,942 in tie-down roping, and the remaining $4,681 scattered in other roping events.

Bareback Riding ✦ Many contestants and spectators consider bareback riding the wildest and most physically demanding of all the contests. Contestants ride a bucking horse for eight seconds, holding nothing but a single-hand-hold rigging cinched around the girth of the horse. The rigging is often described as a sort of suitcase handle.

A rider is disqualified if he touches his equipment, himself, or the horse with his free hand, or is bucked off before the eight-second whistle.

Half of the cowboy's score comes from his spurring technique and "exposure" to the strength of the horse; the other half of his score is determined by the bucking strength and agility of the horse. One other qualification: the rider must have both spurs over the broncs shoulders on the first jump out of the chutes. If the cowboy fails to do this, it is called "missing him out."

Because bareback riding was never really a part of the original rodeo competition, it has often been thought of as an "extra." But in fact, even in the early days cowboys frequently rode unsaddled broncs, often on a dare to prove even more definitively their riding skills. But there is no question that bareback riding as an arena event was a latecomer. At first the rider only held on to the horse's mane. Later a loose rope around the horse's mid-section became the handhold. Then a two-handed cinch that was set up on the horse's withers was developed to make bareback bronc riding a little easier and a little more competitive.

By 1932, a few years after the other events had become standardized, bareback riding became a competitive event at most rodeos, and the single-handed rigging—far more difficult than the two-handed style—became standard.

RIGHT: An early photo of Bill Huntington (left), the inventor of the bareback rigging, and George Williams (right), one of the early masters of rigging riding. Courtesy of the Professional Rodeo Cowboys Association.

In 1940, bareback rider Pete Dixon designed a rigging with the appearance of a suitcase handle. The Dixon rig let the cowboy have better balance and a tighter grip. That rigging has evolved into today's even stiffer hand-hold made of layers of rawhide.

The first bareback champ was Smoky Snyder of Bellflower, California, in 1932. In 2005, Will Lowe of Canyon, Texas, set the money record by winning $185,486 during the season. The highest bareback score was a ninety-four recorded by Wes Stevenson in 2002 and Will Lowe in 2003, both on Kesler Rodeo horses.

Steer Wrestling ✦ According to the PRCA, the concept of steer wrestling seems "straightforward enough"—drop from a horse, grab a steer by the horns, and wrestle it to the ground, stopping the clock as quickly as possible. But like everything to do with rodeo, it's much easier said than done.

BELOW: Steve Dollarhide of Wikieup, Arizona, rides #245 "Lonesome Me Skoal" at the 1992 Calgary Stampede. Photo by Mike Copeman, courtesy of the Professional Rodeo Cowboys Association.

In fact, steer wrestling generally requires a very big cowboy. Few are lighter than 200 pounds or shorter than six feet tall, and the competition is so difficult that no champion has won two consecutive titles since Ote Berry of Checotah, Oklahoma, captured back-to-back crowns in 1990–91.

Timing, technique, strength, and the horsemanship of the hazer (who helps to keep the steer from running straight for the cowboy) are the primary skills needed to succeed.

The first Steer Wrestling champion was Gene Ross of Sayre, Oklahoma, in 1929. Lee Graves of Calgary, Alberta, set the single-season winnings record in 2005 with $206,415.

The fastest time ever recorded was 2.2 seconds by Oral Zumwalt in the 1930s, before a barrier was used. With today's barrier (this gives the steer a slight head start), the fastest time is 2.4 seconds by Jim Bynum and Todd Whatley in 1955, and Gene Melton and Carl Deaton in 1976.

Team Roping ✦
Team roping is the only event that requires the equal participation of two cowboys. It requires precise timing and great anticipation between the header and the heeler and is rodeo's only real team competition. The header has to rope the Mexican Corriente steer around the horns, neck, or a horn-neck combination. He then turns the steer to the left so that the heeler can ride in and rope both of the steer's hind legs. The clock is started when the header leaves the box and it stops when both the cowboy's ropes are taut and their horses are facing each other. In some rodeos, there is a barrier at the heeler's box as well as the header's.

If the heeler catches only one leg instead of two, there is a five-second penalty. If the header doesn't allow the steer to have its allotted head start, or "breaks the barrier," the team receives a ten-second penalty.

The first team roping champion was Charles Maggini of San Jose, California, in 1929. Records distinguishing between headers and heelers were not kept until 1942. In 2005, header Clay Tryan of Billings, Montana, and his partner, heeler Patrick Smith of Midland, Texas, set the season record when they each won $167,204. The world record is held by Blaine Linaweaver and Jory Levy, who roped their steer in 3.5 seconds at San Angelo, Texas, in 2001. That record was tied again by Clay Tryan and Patrick Smith at the 2005 Wrangler NFR.

Saddle Bronc Riding ✦
Saddle bronc is still referred to as rodeo's "classic" event, in part because it truly harkens back to the old days of the early range and trail drives where ranch cowboys would test themselves against one another as they tried to ride the rankest of the unbroken horses in any particular remuda. Saddle bronc riding was also one of the first two events that made up the earliest rodeos. In fact, the event wasn't even called saddle bronc riding until the 1920s. Until bareback riding came on the scene, everyone knew that bronc riders used a saddle and what they did was simply bronc riding.

BELOW: Bill Darnell of Animas, New Mexico, and Jerrold Camarillo of Oakdale, California, both multiple NFR contestants, team roping at Black Jack, Missouri, in 1971.

The first saddle bronc champion was Earl Thode of Belvedere, South Dakota, in 1929. The highest scores on a saddle bronc are ninety-five points by Doug Vold on a horse called "Airwolf" at Innisfall, Alberta, in 1979, and by Glen O'Neill, another Canadian, at Meadow Lake in 1996 on a horse called "Transport."

Rod Warren, a Canadian cowboy from Big Valley, Alberta, completed three straight years of winning the average at the NFR in 2005. In those three years he was never bucked off his bronc. His streak is still intact. The 2005 overall winner was Jeffery Willert of Belvedere, South Dakota, who set a single season earnings record by winning $278,169 for the year.

Tie-Down Roping → This is the event that used to be called "calf roping" until January 2003. A mounted cowboy gives a calf weighing about 250 pounds a headstart, the length determined by the size of the arena. He then chases the calf down the arena. After roping the calf, the rider dismounts, runs down his rope—which is tied hard and fast to his saddle—flanks the calf onto its side, and then ties any three legs with his "piggin' " string that he carries clenched between his teeth.

Everett Bowman of Hillside, Arizona, was the first calf-roping champion in 1929. In 2005, ProRodeo Hall of Famer Fred Whitfield of Hockley, Texas, won his seventh world title with winnings of $168,782. Cody Ohl from Hico, Texas, another multiple world champion, is one of two ropers who own the world record of 6.5 seconds. Ohl achieved that time at the NFR in 2003, and Clint Robinson equaled Ohl's time in 2004.

Little has changed today in saddle bronc riding. The cowboy still has to mount a bucking horse and the competition between man and horse hasn't changed in well over 150 years.

In rodeo competition the bronc rider must start the ride with his feet placed over the shoulders of the bronc on the first jump out of the chutes, just like in bareback riding. The cowboy holds on with a braided rein. If the hold on the rein is too short, the rider can be pulled over the top of the horse; if the rein is too long the rider has no control. One of the keys to saddle bronc riding is the ability to synchronize your spurring action with the horse's bucking style. You also have to stay on for an eight-second trip. Two judges score the rider and the horse. During the ride the cowboy cannot touch the horse with his free hand or kick free of his stirrups.

After the tie is complete, the cowboys must remount and then give the rope slack for six seconds. If the calf does not kick free, it's a legal time.

Dean Oliver calf roping at Red Bluff, California, 1956.

The unpredictable element, though, is that a bull usually weighs up to a ton and always seems to be in a bad mood.

Bull Riding ⤳ It's been said that bull riding is the easiest of all the rodeo events to understand. The rules are simple enough—a cowboy tries to stay on the back of a bull weighing nearly 2,000 pounds for an eight-second ride, holding on to a rope wrapped around the bull's midsection. Other than that, just don't fall off and don't hit the bull with your free hand. Like the other rough stock events, two judges score the rider and the bull, awarding a total of 100 points.

The unpredictable element, though, is that a bull usually weighs up to a ton and always seems to be in a bad mood. The Professional Bull Riders' universal success attests to the excitement that this event creates.

John Schneider of Livermore, California, won the first bull-riding championship in 1929. In 2005, Matt Austin, a cowboy from Wills Point, Texas, won $320,766 to break the single-year earnings record of $297,896 set in 1993 by Ty Murray (one of the greatest rough stock riders to ever compete in the PRCA and a record-setting seven-time All-Around Champion). Murray set the record by competing in three events. Austin, twenty-three years old and a former college cowboy, won all of his money by competing only in bull riding, a truly remarkable feat.

The world record in bull riding was set with the unbelievable perfect score of 100, achieved by Wade Leslie in 1991. Denny Flynn scored a 98 in 1979 and Don Gay had a 97 in 1977.

ABOVE: Jim Shoulders on bull #29 at Cheyenne as the bullfighter gets ready to move in, 1955.

Steer Roping ✦

Steer roping is one of the two original events of rodeo. It came about as part of the skills a good range cowboy had to have. Most of the early cowboys could catch a steer with their rope, but after that they had to find a way to get that animal to the ground so that they could do the work—usually doctoring—that they had roped the steer for in the first place.

In modern steer roping, the only legal catch is around the horns that are protected with horn wraps. After the steer is caught, the roper tosses the slack rope over the steer's right hip and rides to the left, bringing the steer to the ground. Once the steer is on the ground, the roper dismounts and runs to the animal and ties any three legs. As in tie-down roping, after remounting, the roper must give the steer some slack, and if it remains tied for six seconds, it is a legal tie.

Despite the fact that steer roping is one of the oldest rodeo events, it is not held at a majority of rodeos because, as the PRCA points out, it requires large arenas. To be perfectly honest, steer roping, because it is perceived to be harmful to the animal, has actually been banned in some states. The present rules, however, make sure that any alleged cruelty to the steer does not take place. There seems to be a growing acceptance of steer roping as the public comes to understand the safeguards for the steers.

Charles Maggini, the team roping champion of 1929, was also the steer roping winner that same year. Jim Bob Altizer, Sonny Davis, Everett Shaw, Troy Fort, Olin Young, and Shoat Webster all preceded one of the greats of professional rodeo—Guy Allen. In 1998, eighteen-time world champion in this event, Guy Allen won $87,927, a regular-season record and an enormous amount of money in an event that has far fewer opportunities to compete than the other seven regular PRCA contests. It is fitting that Allen also owns the world record of 7.9 seconds, scored in 2000. There are very few athletes, in any sport, that so dominate their event as Allen does. He has gone to the National Steer Roping Finals twenty-nine consecutive years (a PRCA record) and was inducted into the ProRodeo Hall of Fame in 1996. Allen is formerly of New Mexico and now lives in Santa Anna, Texas. It is easy to understand why he is referred to by his fellow cowboys as "The Legend."

OPPOSITE: Guy Allen, the most dominant figure in steer roping, shows his form. Photo courtesy of Jennings Photography.

RIGHT: Jimmie Gibbs Monroe was an intercollegiate champion from Sam Houston State and the World Champion in 1975 and 1976. She is seen here running the barrels at the NFR. In 1992 she was inducted into the National Cowgirl Hall of Fame. Photo by Springer, courtesy of Jimmie Gibbs Monroe.

Barrel Racing ✦

Barrel racing is the only event for women on the regular PRCA tour. It is a show of real horsemanship. The rules are not very complicated. The cowgirl must run a cloverleaf pattern around three barrels set in a big triangle. The rider can do the pattern in either direction and she is penalized five seconds for each barrel that she knocks over.

Most of the cowgirls use quarter horses, and speed and agility are the two main requirements for the horse. For the rider, balance and a feeling of unison with the horse are absolute. In this event, horse and rider are true partners.

There are no world records for this event, only arena records, because the size of the pattern is determined by the size of the arena and they vary greatly. This is also the only event that has no judges beyond the one that counts—the clock. Today's races are so close that they are timed to the hundredth of a second.

Margaret Owens was the Women's Professional Rodeo Association top barrel racer in 1948 when the women started to keep their own records. In 2005, the Texas cowgirl Kelly Kaminski won her second title with year-end winnings of $191,702, and she was the only 2004 world champion who was able to defend her title at the 2005 Wrangler NFR. In between Margaret Owens and Kelly Kaminski, the gal many consider to be the greatest barrel racer of all time dominated the sport. Cowgirl Charmayne James, formerly of Clayton, New Mexico, won eleven world titles, almost all of them riding her equally famous quarter horse, "Scamper."

The
Cowboy

Way

Allen Houston behind the chutes, getting ready for the saddle bronc competition in Scottsdale, Arizona, 1964. Photo courtesy of Louise L. Serpa, Tucson, Arizona.

Over the years rodeo has changed. It isn't the same sport it was in the 1920s and '30s or after World War II, and it isn't the sport that it was in the 1970s. There is more money, the competitors think of themselves as athletes and work and train more, fewer contestants come from ranch families, and there are now sponsorships for the individual contestants and for the Professional Rodeo Cowboys Association. Rodeo, at least from one perspective, is beginning to look like all other big-league sports. Included in all the growth is the striking success of the Professional Bull Riders (PBR), an independent group of "toro twisters" who plays before sold-out crowds all over the country.

But rodeo remains a sport for individuals. There still isn't a "rodeo team" concept once you get to the pros, and it hasn't lost its sense of honor and fairness. Despite the increased purses and sponsorships, rodeo still isn't primarily about money. The fact that the better contestants can make a good living doing what they obviously enjoy doing is certainly a positive part of today's sport, and rodeo still remains a place for individualism and the one thing that nearly every one of the competitors craves—independence. When you have a sport that allows you to pick and choose where you want to compete, when you want to compete, and how you want to compete, you have independence that few professional athletes have or will ever have. Very few of the thousands who compete will get to wear that gold championship buckle and only a small percentage will even cover their expenses, but they will decide themselves when they want to stop straddling that last bull, or spurring that last bronc, or riding that last cloverleaf pattern.

Why the cowboys and cowgirls continue to participate in this incredibly dangerous sport varies from athlete to athlete. They all have their own stories and they all have their own reasons. But overall, the cowboys and cowgirls of today haven't philosophically changed all that much

from the cowboys of the 1930s who were even afraid to join the Cowboys' Turtle Association because it *might* mean giving up their independence.

Rodeo is as much a way of life as it is a sport. To many people, both fans and contestants, rodeo represents a very romantic way of life. It might seem especially romantic if you are tied down in an office or some job that you don't like. But to most contestants, in addition to it being an exciting and challenging athletic contest, rodeo represents a way of connecting with a tradition and history that they admire and respect. The "cowboy way" and "cowboy up" are not just phrases to the men and women on the rodeo circuit. They are themes to live by.

ABOVE: World Champion Saddle Bronc Rider Billy Etbauer on "Roan Wolf," owned by Charlie Battle Rodeo Company of Texas at Cheyenne Frontier Days. Etbauer is one of three Etbauer saddle bronc riders, all NFR contestants. Brothers Robert and Dan are retired. Photo by Jennings, courtesy of the Professional Rodeo Cowboys Association.

LEFT: Bob Ragsdale, former PRCA president, calf roping (tie-down roping) in the mud at Red Bluff, California in 1965. Courtesy of the Professional Rodeo Cowboys Association.

☙ Bibliography ☙

Adams, Andy. *The Log of a Cowboy.* Boston: Houghton Mifflin Company, 1936.

Allard, William Albert. *Vanishing Breed: Photographs of the Cowboy and the West.* Boston: Little, Brown and Company, 1982.

Atherton, Lewis. *The Cattle Kings.* Bloomington: Indiana University Press, 1967.

Bartlett, Richard A. *The New Country: A Social History of the American Frontier 1776–1890.* New York: Oxford University Press, 1974.

Bernstein, Joel H. *Families That Take in Friends: An Informal History of Dude Ranching.* Stevensville, Montana: Stoneydale Press, 1982.

Bowman, John S., ed. *The World Almanac of the American West.* New York: World Almanac, 1986.

Bowman, R. Lewis. *Bumfuzzled.* Bisbee, Arizona: R. Lewis Bowman, 1995.

———. *Bumfuzzled Too.* Bisbee, Arizona: R. Lewis Bowman, 2000.

Bramlett, Jim. *Ride for the High Points: The Real Story of Will James.* Missoula, Montana: Mountain Press Publishing Company, 1987.

Brown, J.P.S. *The Outfit: A Cowboy's Primer.* New York: The Dial Press, 1971.

Bryant, Tom, and Joel H. Bernstein. *A Taste of Ranching: Cooks and Cowboys.* Albuquerque: Border Books, 1993.

———. *A Taste of Texas Ranching: Cooks and Cowboys.* Lubbock, Texas: Texas Tech University Press, 1995.

Burk, Dale. *A Brush with the West.* Missoula, Montana: Mountain Press Publishing Company, 1980.

Campion, Lynn. *Rodeo.* Guilford, Connecticut: The Lyons Press, 2002.

Clancy, Foghorn. *My Fifty Years in Rodeo,* San Antonio; The Naylor Company, 1952.

Crandall, Judy. *Cowgirls: Early Images and Collectibles.* Atglen, Pennsylvania: Schiffer Publishing Ltd., 1994.

Dary, David. *Cowboy Culture: A Saga of Five Centuries.* Lawrence: University Press of Kansas, 1989.

Dawson, Patrick. *Mr. Rodeo: The Big Bronc Years of Leo Crèmer.* Livingston, Montana: Cayuse Press, 1986.

Duncan, Dayton. *Out West: An American Journey.* New York: Viking, 1987.

Dusard, Jay, and Thomas McGuane. *Horses.* Tucson: Rio Nuevo Publishers, 2005.

Editors of Time-Life Books, text by Paul O'Neil. *The End of the Myth.* Alexandria, Virginia: Time-Life Books, 1979.

Fenin, George N., and William K. Everson. *The Western: From Silents to the Seventies.* New York: Penguin Books, 1973.

Flynn, Shirley E. *Let's Go, Let's Show, Let's Rodeo: The History of Cheyenne Frontier Days.* Cheyenne, Wyoming: Wigwam Publishing Company, 1996.

Frantz, Joe B., and Julian Ernest Choate, Jr. *The American Cowboy: The Myth and the Reality.* Norman: University of Oklahoma Press, 1955.

Fredrikson, Kristine. *American Rodeo: From Buffalo Bill to Big Business.* College Station: Texas A&M University Press, 1985.

Freeman, Danny. *World's Oldest Rodeo.* Prescott, Arizona: Prescott Frontier Days Inc./Classic Printers, 1988.

Furlong, Charles Wellington. *Let 'Er Buck: A Story of the Passing of the Old West.* New York: G. P. Putnam's Sons, 1921.

Furnas, J. C. *The Americans: A Social History of the United States, 1587–1914.* New York: G. P. Putnam's Sons, 1969.

Geist, Valerius. *Buffalo Nation: History and Legend of the North American Bison.* Stillwater, Minnesota: Voyageur Press, 1996.

Gilchriest, Gail. *The Cowgirl Companion.* New York: Hyperion, 1993.

Green, Douglas B. *Singing in the Saddle: The History of the Singing Cowboy.* Nashville: The Country Music Foundation Press & Vanderbilt University Press, 2002.

Hadley, Drum. *Voices of the Borderland.* Tucson: Rio Nuevo Publishers, 2005.

Hassrick, Royal B. *Cowboys and Indians: An Illustrated History.* London: Octopus Books Limited, 1976.

Hine, Robert V. *The American West: An Interpretive History.* Boston: Little, Brown and Company, 1973.

Honour, Hugh. *The European Vision of America.* Cleveland: The Cleveland Museum of Art, 1975.

Jordan, Teresa. *Rodeo History and Legends.* Montrose, Colorado: Rodeo Stuff, 1994.

———. *Cowgirls: Women of the American West.* New York: Anchor Press, 1982.

Jory, Doug and Kathy. *From Pendleton to Calgary.* Pendleton, Oregon: Outpost #1, 2002.

———. *Oregon Cowboy Country.* Hines, Oregon: Outpost #1, 2005.

———. *The Badlands.* Hines, Oregon: Outpost #1, 2004.

Kesey, Ken, with Ken Babbs. *Last Go Round: A Real Western.* New York: Penguin Books, 1994.

Lamar, Howard R. *Charlie Siringo's West: An Interpretive Biography.* Albuquerque: University of New Mexico Press, 2005.

Lamb, Gene. *Rodeo Back of the Chutes.* Denver: Bell Press, 1955.

Lawrence, Elizabeth Atwood. *Rodeo: An Anthropologist Looks at the Wild and the Tame.* Chicago: The University of Chicago Press, 1984.

LeCompte, Mary Lou. *Cowgirls of the Rodeo: Pioneer Professional Athletes.* Chicago: University of Illinois Press, 1993.

Logsdon, Guy, Mary Roger and William Jacobson. *Saddle Serenaders.* Salt Lake City: Gibbs Smith, Publisher, 1995.

Marvine, Dee. *The Lady Rode Bucking Horses.* Guilford, Connecticut: Two Dot, 2005.

The West of Buffalo Bill. Introduction by Dr. Harold McCracken. New York: Harry N. Abrams Inc., 1974.

O'Connor, Sandra Day, and H. Alan Day. *Lazy B: Growing Up on a Cattle Ranch in the American Southwest.* New York: Random House, 2002.

Porter, Willard H. *Who's Who in Rodeo.* Oklahoma City: Powder River Book Company, 1982.

Riske, Milt. *Those Magnificent Cowgirls: A History of the Rodeo Cowgirl.* Cheyenne: Wyoming Publishing, 1983.

Rupp, Virgil. *Let 'Er Buck: A History of the Pendleton Round-Up.* Pendleton, Oregon: Pendleton Round-Up Association/Master Printers, 1985.

Ryan, Kathleen. *Ranching Traditions.* New York: Cross River Press, 1989.

Scriver, Bob. *An Honest Try.* Kansas City: The Lowell Press, 1975.

Serpa, Louise. *Rodeo.* New York: Aperture, 1994.

Siringo, Charles A. *A Texas Cowboy: Fifteen Years on the Hurricane Deck of a Spanish Pony.* Lincoln: University of Nebraska Press, 1979.

Stratton, W. K. *Chasing the Rodeo.* New York: Harcourt, Inc., 2005.

Streep, Peg. *Cowgirl Rising: The Art of Donna Howell-Sickles.* Shelton, Connecticut: The Greenwich Workshop Press, 1997.

Taylor, Joshua C. *America as Art.* New York: Harper & Row, Publishers, 1976.

Van Cleve, Spike. *40 Years' Gatherin's.* Kansas City: The Lowell Press, 1977.

Wallis, Michael. *The Real Wild West: The 101 Ranch and the Creation of the American West.* New York: St. Martin's Press, 1999.

Ward, Fay E. *The Working Cowboy's Manual.* New York: Bonanza Books, 1983.

Webb, Walter Prescott. *The Great Frontier.* Austin: University of Texas Press, 1964.

Westermeier, Clifford P. *Man, Beast, Dust: The Story of Rodeo.* Lincoln: University of Nebraska Press, 1987.

Wister, Owen. *The Virginian.* New York: The Macmillan Co., 1902.

Woerner, Gail Hughbanks. *Belly Full of Bedsprings: The History of Bronc Riding.* Austin, Texas: Eakin Press, 1998.

———. *Fearless Funnymen: The History of the Rodeo Clown.* Austin, Texas: Eakin Press, 1993.

Wooden, Wayne S., and Gavin Ehringer. *Rodeo in America: Wranglers, Roughstock & Paydirt.* Lawrence: University of Kansas Press, 1996.

Zarzyski, Paul, and Barbara Van Cleve. *Roughstock Sonnets.* Kansas City: The Lowell Press, 1989.

———. *All This Way for the Short Ride.* Santa Fe: Museum of New Mexico Press, 1996.

Calgary Stampede: The Greatest Outdoor Show on Earth, VHS. Calgary, Alberta: Calgary Stampede, n.d.

Let 'er Buck: Rodeo—The Early Years, Volume 1. VHS. Scottsdale, AZ: Longhorn Media Productions, 1994.